UNDERSTANDING MARKETING
A EUROPEAN CASEBOOK

GE

UNDERSTANDING MARKETING
A EUROPEAN CASEBOOK

by

Celia Phillips
London School of Economics

Ad Pruyn
Rotterdam School of Management

Marie-Paule Kestemont
Université Catholique de Louvain

JOHN WILEY & SONS, LTD
Chichester • New York • Weinheim • Brisbane • Singapore • Toronto

Copyright © 2000 John Wiley & Sons, Ltd,
Baffins Lane, Chichester,
West Sussex PO19 1UD, England

National   01243 779777
International (+44) 1243 779777
e-mail (for orders and customer service enquiries): cs-books@wiley.co.uk
Visit our Home Page on http://www.wiley.co.uk
or http://www.wiley.com

Other Wiley Editorial Offices

John Wiley & Sons, Inc., 605 Third Avenue,
New York, NY 10158-0012, USA

WILEY-VCH Verlag GmbH, Pappelallee 3,
D-69469 Weinheim, Germany

Jacaranda Wiley Ltd, 33 Park Road, Milton,
Queensland 4064, Australia

John Wiley & Sons (Asia) Pte Ltd, 2 Clementi Loop #02-01,
Jin Xing Distripark, Singapore 129809

John Wiley & Sons (Canada) Ltd, 22 Worcester Road,
Rexdale, Ontario M9W 1L1, Canada

Library of Congress Cataloging-in-Publication Data

Phillips, Celia.
Understanding marketing : a European casebook / by Celia Phillips, Ad Pruyn, Marie Paule-Kestemont.
p. cm.
Includes bibliographical references and index.
ISBN 0-471-86093-X
1. Marketing—Europe—Case studies. 2. Export marketing—Europe—Case studies.
I. Pruyn, Ad. II. Paule-Kestemont, Marie. III. Title.
HF5415.12.E8 P48 2000
658.8'0094—dc21

99–059517

British Library Cataloguing in Publication Data

A catalogue record for this book is available from the British Library

ISBN 0-471-86093-X

Typeset in 11/13pt Garamond by Mayhew Typesetting, Rhayader, Powys
Printed and bound in Great Britain by Bookcraft (Bath) Ltd, Midsomer Norton
This book is printed on acid-free paper responsibly manufactured from sustainable forestry, in which at least two trees are planted for each one used for paper production.

Contents

Contributors

Per Andersson is Assistant Professor at Stockholm School of Economics. He has participated in research projects on industry dynamics and industrial distribution with focus on the automotive industry, mechanical engineering and biotechnology.

Josef Berács is Professor of Marketing at the Budapest University of Economic Sciences, and is chair of the department.

Mogens Bjerre is a management consultant with COGISYS A/S and PA. A former student of the Copenhagen Business School, he has authored and co-authored books on franchising, trade marketing and branding.

Marc Brenneiser is Assistant Professor at the Seminar for Business Management, Market Research and Marketing, Cologne University. He studied business management from 1987 to 1993. In his doctoral thesis he is working on the Development and Implementation of Marketing Strategies for Consumer Goods Markets in the People's Republic of China.

Anina Busch is a member of the Marketing Faculty of the University of St Gallen.

Yvonne van Everdingen is a member of the Marketing Faculty at Erasmus University, Rotterdam.

Axel Faix is Assistant Professor at the Seminar for Business Management, Market Research and Marketing, Cologne University, where he teaches Market Research. He studied business administration from

1985 to 1991 (Dipl-Kfm) and received his doctor's degree at Cologne University in 1998. His research topics are in the area of strategic marketing, marketing organization and innovation management.

Josep Franch, Licenciatura and MBA degrees in Business Administration, ESADE, is Associate Professor of Marketing at ESADE in Barcelona. He was previously a resident researcher, IMD (Lausanne, Switzerland) 1996 to 1997. He is a marketing consultant and specialist in international marketing and relationship marketing.

Franz Habann studied business administation at the Universities of Bayreuth and Cologne from 1984 to 1991 (Dipl-Kfm). From 1991 to 1994 he was a research specialist at McKinsey & Co., Dusseldorf. From 1994 to 1999 he worked as Assistant Professor at the Seminar for Business Administration, Market Research and Marketing at Cologne University. He received his doctor's degree in 1998. Since 1999 Dr Frank Habann has been a project manager and lecturer at the Institute for Media and Communications Management, University of St Gallen.

Staffan Hultén is a member of the faculty at the Stockholm School of Economics.

Hans Hüttemann, who received his doctor's degree at Cologne University, is Assistant Professor at the Seminar for Business Management, Market Research and Marketing, Cologne University. His research interests revolve around marketing decision models and the design and analysis of experiments for marketing decisions.

Anne Christin Kemper studied business administration from 1988 to 1993 at the University of Munster. Since 1993, she has been Assistant Professor at the Seminar for Business Management, Market Research and Marketing, Cologne University, where she teaches Marketing Accounting. Her doctoral thesis deals with branding in industrial markets. Further subjects of her research include strategic marketing, industrial and services marketing, and organizational buying behaviour.

Marie-Paule Kestemont is Professor of Marketing at the University of Louvain.

Richard Köhler has been Director of the Seminar for Business Management, Market research and Marketing ("Marketing Seminar") at Cologne University since 1979. Between 1973 and 1979 he was Director of the Institute for Economic Sciences at the Technical University of Aachen. Before that he taught at Mannheim University. He has practical experience in the fields of banking, public accounting and marketing-consulting. Prof. Köhler has been a member of the CEMS Interfaculty Group on Marketing since 1990.

Robert Kozielski is an Assistant Professor at the University of Lodz in the Department of Marketing. He is also a member of the KLG Marketing group.

Hanna Machkova is a Seminar Lecturer at the Prague University of Economics where she is Director of the French-Czech Institute of Management. Recent publications include *A Dictionary of Management* (HZ Praha, 1995), with Boyer and Hronova, *Urban S. Europe in Progress, Model & Facts* (Gabler, 1995) and *S. Europe's Economic Future* (Gabler, 1994).

Ron Meyer, is Assistant Professor of Strategic Management at the Erasmus University's Rotterdam School of Management. He is co-author of a leading strategic marketing textbook and managing director of the consulting and training company De Wit and Meyer Strategy Works.

Bengt G. Mölleryd is an analyst at AB Stellocom, Sweden. He was previously a PhD student at the Stockholm School of Economics, Department of Marketing, Distribution and Industry Dynamics, where he was part of the project "Telecommunications: An Industry in Transformation". His research concerns the role of entrepreneurship in the development of large technological systems such as mobile telecommunications.

Jordi Montaña is a Professor of Marketing at ESADE in Barcelona.

Joachim Mühlmeyer is a member of the Marketing Faculty of the University of St Gallen.

Jana Nagyova is a member of the faculty of International Relations at Prague University of Economics and the Czech Management Center,

Graduate School of Business in Celakovice in the Czech Republic. Publications include several university textbooks, and the marketing section in the Logos Multilingual Dictionary.

Celia Phillips is Senior Tutor at the Interdisciplinary Institute of Management at the London School of Economics; she is a Social Statistician. Her doctorate was in the area of comparative education and subsequent publications have been in areas including violence in the workplace, and statistical sources of civil aviation. She wrote the case on shopping centres in the European case studies book "Cases in Marketing", edited by H.H. Larsen (Sage, 1997).

Ad Pruyn is a member of the Marketing Faculty at Erasmus University, Rotterdam.

Krzysztof Przybylowski is an Assistant Professor at the Warsaw School of Economics. Publications include case studies and articles in the marketing area and a textbook, *A Set of Questions on the Principles of Marketing* (Foundation of Education, Lodz, 1994).

Alexander Roosdorp was formerly a member of the Marketing Faculty at the University of St Gallen.

Thomas Rudolph is a member of the Marketing Faculty at the University of St Gallen.

Rudolph Sinkovics is a faculty member of the International Marketing and Management Department of Wirtschaftsuniversität, Vienna.

Barbara Stöttinger is a faculty member of the International Marketing and Management Department of Wirtschaftsuniversität, Vienna.

Valerie Swaen is a researcher at the University of Louvain.

Foreword

The Community of European Management Schools (CEMS) Inter-faculty Group on Marketing has now produced its third book of practical case studies. The first was edited by Jordi Montaña (ESADE, Barcelona); the second by our beloved colleague, the late Hanne Hartvig Larsen (Copenhagen Business School); and the third one is edited by Celia Phillips (London School of Economics), Ad Pruyn (Rotterdam School of Management) and Marie-Paul Kestemont Université Catholique de Louvain (Louvain-la-Neuve).

The book is a collection of short marketing cases designed for use in multi-cultural environments. It is academically sound, but simultaneously entertaining and easy to read. Among the contributors are a number of prominent academics from the leading European management schools.

I would like to congratulate Celia Phillips, Ad Pruyn and Marie-Paul Kestemont for the fine job they have done (we all know how hard it is to coordinate the work of so many academics) and thank all the other authors for their contributions.

I am certain that this third book of marketing cases will be a great success.

Carlo-Maria Gallucci
ESADE
Chair, CEMS IFG Group on Marketing

Preface

Some two years ago members of the Interfaculty Marketing group of the Community of European Management Schools (CEMS) agreed to produce a collection of short marketing cases which were to be used in the classroom on the spot rather than involving students in extensive preparatory work.

We feel our colleagues have done us proud. Their cases are fresh and varied and, we hope, give some "feel" of the directions being taken by European marketing. Each case has an introduction written by Celia Phillips.

Points worth noting are

- The *geographical* coverage of the cases. The contributions cover 14 countries and include some that are Europe-wide. We are particularly happy to present five cases from former "Soviet bloc" countries.
- The *variety* of topics covered. As the Introduction shows, the cases come from a wide area of marketing topics. We feel they could be used for consumer and industrial marketing courses as well as general or international marketing.
- The availability of updated *teaching notes*. An important aspect of this collection of cases lies in the teaching notes which are available on the Internet to course conveners only. These give further background information, ideas for approaching the questions and suggestions for organizing class-work based on the writers' experience with their cases. It is intended that they will be regularly updated where appropriate.

We hope that users of the cases, both lecturers and students alike, will enjoy the cases and find they do indeed help to understand marketing.

We should like to thank all of our colleagues for their help over the years. In particular Helen Cagnoni for her encouragement and assistance in the compilation of this book.

Celia Phillips
Ad Pruyn
Marie-Paule Kestemont
September 1999

Introduction

Celia Phillips

While there are many good marketing texts currently on the market, teachers of general marketing courses eventually find they have run out of short, up-to-date, cases – particularly those written from a European perspective. This collection attempts to remedy this. The 20 cases, all recent and some current, come from 14 countries and faculty members of 14 European universities. They are designed to be worked on on the spot and require two, or at most three, hours of class time.

The cases are designed to cover subject material in six sections commonly presented in student texts:

- *Strategic marketing*, by which we mean the examination of the marketing issues and decisions which need to be made in a particular scenario and their impact at the different stages in the marketing process
- *Branding and brand positioning*, which covers discussions of brand stretching
- *New products and new technologies* are such an important category within the general product area that we feel they deserve a category of their own
- *Business to business, cooperation and competition*
- *Communication and promotion*
- *Product, price and distribution*

Any grouping is arbitrary but we hope that teachers will find this one helpful. The headings incorporate the "four Ps" to some extent.

We have added "strategic marketing" and "business to business" as categories in their own right. The former should, of course, underpin any marketing case, while the latter is of increasing interest. We have subdivided "product" into two categories – "branding" and "new products" – to reflect the balance of the cases. We feel that ideas of product development which incorporate new technologies should be studied in their own right. "Promotion" covers the usual topics. We have combined "price" and "place" in the category "product, price and distribution" because, in the cases presented here, they seemed to go together.

The Introductory table (*see* p. xvii) shows how each case falls into these categories from the point of view of its main subject matter and its focus. It can be seen that some of the cases have more than one focus, and it is these which might repay the spending of more than the minimum class time recommended.

It is worth noting some other aspects of the cases which are not covered by the tables. Three cases, numbers 8 (on the benzene crisis), 11 (on OXFAM policies) and 15 (on alcopops), deal to some extent with the place of ethical issues in marketing. Two cases, numbers 12 (on banking) and 20 (on emergency services), deal with the service sector. Finally, case 20 is an extremely useful market research case.

It is hoped that the cases are all reasonably accessible to a cursory glance before detailed work is undertaken. Each begins with a brief introduction which highlights the main points: main and subsidiary focus, scene, main players, and product are given to help provide an overview. In addition, each case contains an indexed keyword list to enable readers to look for any particular topics they may wish to concentrate on. Finally, each case gives questions for discussion related to the areas shown in the Introductory table, and references for further study.

Prices, revenue and market share are all given in the currency of the country of the case concerned. This is translated into both Euros and American dollars for the first figures given. After that, readers will need to refer to the list of conversions given in the Currency table on p. xviii.

As described in the Preface, both teaching notes and an update on the cases will be available to teachers on the Internet. More detailed

INTRODUCTORY TABLE   Case numbers classified by main subject and focus

	1	2	3	4	5	6	7	8	9	10	11	12	13	14	15	16	17	18	19	20
Strategic marketing	M	F	F			F	F	F		F	M		M	M		F	F		F	
Branding/brand positioning				F			M						F					M		
New products/new technologies					M	F			M	M		M			M				F	
Business to business/cooperation and competition			M		F				F			F	F							M
Communication/promotion				M	F	M		M	F							M		F	M	
Product, price and distribution	F	M	F	F	F	F		F	F	F			F			F	M	F	F	

M, main subject; F, focus.

CURRENCY TABLE For currencies used in cases (August 1999)

Country	Currency	Equivalent of 100 of currency	
		in Euros	in US dollars
Austria	Schilling (ATS)	7.27	4.78
Czech Republic	Koruna (CZK)	2.82	1.91
European Union	Euro		105.81
Germany	Deutschmark (DM)	51.13	54.10
Hungary	Forint	0.41	0.44
Netherlands	Guilder (DFL)	45.38	48.01
Norway	Krone	12.14	12.69
Poland	Zloty (zl.)	25.03	26.81
Spain	Peseta (PTA)	0.60	0.64
Sweden	Krona	11.59	12.11
Switzerland	Swiss franc (CHF)	62.15	66.09
UK	Pound (£)	152.02	161.85
USA	Dollar ($)	94.51	

discussion on the lengths and allocation of time advised for each case and on appropriate teaching methods is given there.

Acknowledgements

The Publisher wishes to thank the following companies for use of material.

AC Nielsen
Association of Hungarian Breweries
Bass
Beiersdorf AG
Budapest University of Economic Sciences
Canadead Limited
CMBC
Coca-Cola
De Wit and Meyer
Hamon, A.
Hospodarske Noviny
HVG
Intermediar
International Committee of the Red Cross

Management Zentrum, St Gallen
MD Foods
Mediagnózis
Migros-Genoussenschafts-Bund
Mintel International Group Ltd
Oxfam
Petrobank
Prague Breweries
Rzeczpospolita
Schwarzkopf & Henkel
Statistical Yearbook of Hungary
Wýzkumý ústav pivovarský a sladařský
Young and Rubicam

The publisher will be glad to hear from any copyright holders whom it has not been possible to to contact.

1

The mobile telephone supplier: choosing a channel entry strategy

Per Andersson and Bengt G. Mölleryd

Case	Strategic marketing
Main focus	Market entry, business to business
Subsidiary focus	Distribution, market segmentation
Scene	Sweden, Europe as a whole
Players	Network operators, supplier, retailer, consumer
Product	Mobile telephone

Summary

What choices face a mobile telephone supplier entering a new and highly deregulated telecommunications market? In a situation where the main elements of the distribution system – operations, suppliers, middlemen and customer categories – change continually, how can a telephone supplier enter the international arena with any hope of success?

© 2000 John Wiley & Sons, Ltd.
Understanding Marketing: A European Casebook edited by Celia Phillips, Ad Pruyn and Marie-Paule Kestemont.

Introduction

This is a strategic marketing case with a focus on market entry. We have here a company (Mobicom) which has had reasonable sales in a particular country over a period. It is now on the point of developing a strategy for consolidating its position and taking a larger share in a rapidly changing market. The country chosen is Sweden, interesting in itself as a major mobile telephone market, but readers might like to consider looking at the implications of these findings for such a market entry nearer home.

The authors track the changing relationship between network operator, supplier, retailer and consumer from the early 1970s to the mid 1990s. Over the period, one sees the emergence of three main operators, the rise and fall of a number of suppliers (from six in the 1970s to 20 at their peak in the early 1980s and now down to three), and a proliferation of retailers, which reflects the widening of the market from small companies to groups of public organizations and private consumers.

The questions set arise from the main aspects of the case presented: the effects of structural change in the distribution system coupled with technical changes, the problem of market segmentation – should the company target organizational buyers or private consumers? Underpinning these comes the main question, how do these answers affect a possible choice of market entry strategy? One further question brings us to the present: what further information might be needed to decide on the next entry strategy in the next market?

KEYWORDS

Distribution system, private consumers, organizational buyers, network dynamics, technological change, market entry, marketing strategy, operators, suppliers, retailers.

Case

Jan Olsen, newly appointed Market Area Manager for the Nordic region at the Dutch-German telecommunication and electronic appliances manufacturer Mobicom International, arrived at his office on Monday morning. Within the next two weeks he would have to come up with a plan including a set of alternative strategies for how to strengthen the company's position in the Nordic region. Focus was to be directed towards the Swedish market, as this small but highly deregulated market had been chosen as a "development and test market" for the company's mobile telephone, telecommunication and information technology (IT) related business. In the European marketing organization, Sweden had been chosen as one in a group of important dynamic markets. The high penetration rate of mobile telephony among private and organizational users was one important factor. Mobicom counted on being able to use also in other European markets the experience that it could gain from being positioned in this small market.

On a small scale Mobicom had been providing mobile telephones to a number of scattered retailers and chains on the Swedish market, but the mother company's brand was generally associated with other electronic appliances, including consumer goods like television sets, video recorders and hi-fi equipment. This also included computers. It was known that in the Swedish markets, the company would face severe competition from mobile telephone suppliers such as Ericsson, Motorola and Nokia. However, as in many other markets, it was also well known that the network of firms in the distribution system for mobile telephones included a large number of other important actors: operators, wholesalers, retailers, and of course the consumer and organizational buyers. The emerging technological convergence of telecommunications, IT, media and household appliances made it even more difficult to draw boundaries around the distribution system.

Jan Olsen had promised, at a meeting with the central, pan-European marketing team in Amsterdam, to present a set of alternative marketing channel strategies which would strengthen the mobile telephone division's position in the Swedish and Nordic markets. In practice, due to Mobicom's weak and fairly sporadic sales in the Swedish market, he would essentially have to formulate a set of "new" market entry alternatives. Other issues which had been discussed before the meeting included the question of how the company should handle the increasing polarization between private consumers and organizational users. Among the organizational users, the use of mobile telephones was rapidly becoming part of a large integrated system of solutions for the organization's total information and communication needs.

Jan Olsen had only two weeks to prepare a presentation of a set of alternative marketing channel strategies, including weaknesses and strengths of the different alternatives. These were to be discussed at the meeting with the pan-European marketing team. As the recently appointed manager for the Nordic region, Jan knew the management team would scrutinize his analyses very carefully. As a first step he decided to take a look at a recently performed historical study of the Swedish distribution system for mobile telephones.

BACKGROUND: THE SWEDISH DISTRIBUTION SYSTEM FOR MOBILE TELEPHONES UP TO 1995

Jan Olsen found a description of the overall changes in the Swedish distribution system for mobile telephones between 1971 and 1995 (Andersson and Mölleryd, 1998). A set of descriptive data described the evolution of the distribution system as a complement to this. They are given in Table 1.1.

The basic picture was that, after the period 1971–1986 which had been dominated by Swedish Telecom Radio, between 1986 and 1991, three leading suppliers had begun to emerge: Motorola, Nokia-Mobira and Ericsson. Successively, suppliers had abandoned the idea of exclusivity with strong forward vertical integration with retailers. The general rapid diffusion of mobile telephones put more pressure on the leading players. For example, retailers had been busy handling the growing number of customers, but despite increasing sales of mobile telephones and subscriptions, increasing price competition had resulted in the first serious shakeout of medium-sized, local specialist retailers in 1991.

Two operators had opened up new GSM (Global System for Telecommunications) systems during the first half of the 1990s, competing with Telia Mobitel's NMT (Nordic Mobile Telecommunications) and GSM systems. Motorola, Ericsson and Nokia-Mobira had established themselves as dominating telephone suppliers. Cooperation between suppliers and service operators increased. (Ericsson Radio Systems' and Telia's long-term cooperation in telecommunications had continued, Motorola had developed a pocket telephone to match Telia Mobitel's launching of new NMT services adapted to private consumers, etc.)

TABLE 1.1 Actors in the mobile telephone network, Sweden: changes, 1971–1994

	1971–1981	1981–1986	1986–1991	1991–1994
Network operators	Swedish Telecom, smaller private operators	Comvik, Swedish Telecom Radio	Comvik, Swedish Telecom Radio	Comvik, Europolitan, Telia Mobitel
Suppliers	Six main suppliers: AP, Handic, Mitsubishi, Salora, SRA, Storno	20 suppliers	Seven main suppliers: Ericsson, Motorola, Nokia-Mobira, Panasonic, Philips, Technophone, Mitsubishi	Three major suppliers: Ericsson, Motorola and Nokia-Mobira
Retailers	Mobile telephone specialists	Mobile telephone specialists, car dealers	Mobile telephone specialists, car dealers, office equipment retailers	Mobile telephone specialists, car dealers, office equipment retailers, radio and TV shops, Telia shops
Users	Small companies	Small and medium-sized companies	Small and medium-sized companies, large companies, public organizations	Small and medium-sized companies, large companies, public organizations, private consumers

From 1991, Nokia and Motorola had developed their contacts with retailers. They had directed attention towards the largest retailers and retail chains in the major city regions. Motorola had appointed 25 to 30 so-called "megadealers" while Nokia-Mobira had tied the 20 largest dealers to the organization by developing a new marketing concept, "Mobira Business Partner". Strong links had also been developed between retailers and the service operators Telia Mobitel, Comvik and Europolitan. The organizational contacts with the largest retailers had also changed character. Most large retailers now belonged to retail chains. The three leading suppliers' and the three operators' contacts had been redirected to a central HQ organization, an intermediate level between the supplier or operator and the retail outlets. Powerful retail organizations had developed. Despite this, and as a consequence of the rapid diffusion of mobile telephone sales among radio and TV retailers, a second wave of retailer shakeout had come at the end of 1994 connected with customer type.

New private consumers tended to buy through radio and TV retailers, while company customers had continued to go to the local mobile telephone specialist. In addition, the large company customers had started to establish direct contacts with the operators' newly formed, specialized corporate sales departments, which in turn connected customers to local retailers. Within the largest retail chains a polarization trend had been observed: specialized "tele bars" (small shops for the consumer market) had been opened in the cities, while the internal sales organizations had been adapted to the corporate customers. Large corporate customers had changed purchasing policies, centralizing purchasing to one organizational HQ unit but maintaining localized contacts with local retailers in matters concerning, for example, services.

EMERGING TRENDS AFTER 1995: CHANNEL CONSEQUENCES OF CONTINUED TECHNOLOGICAL CONVERGENCE?

After 1995, two technological trends had begun to put their mark on Swedish marketing channels: (1) the convergence of mobile and fixed telephone systems and services and (2) the convergence of telecommunications and IT systems and services.

There had been increased integration between mobile and fixed telephones, in both hardware and services, starting in the business segment with the introduction of wireless access, integrating fixed and mobile networks. There was also an increased convergence between the mobile telephone and telecommunications and communication technologies. Ericsson, Nokia and Motorola had begun to experience increased competition as new suppliers had entered the Swedish market for mobile telephones (e.g. Sony and Philips).

Established manufacturers in the computer industry had developed contacts with manufacturers and suppliers and distributors in the mobile telephone business. Computers had been prepared for mobile telephone transmission and computer companies had become a direct (via contacts with mobile telephone retailers) or indirect (via contacts with mobile telephone manufacturers) part of the distribution network for mobile telephones. The distribution networks for computer products and services and for mobile telephone products and services had increasingly been interlinked.

GOING FOR PRIVATE CONSUMERS AND/OR ORGANIZATIONAL BUYERS?

An important driving force for channel changes was the rapid take-off of sales to consumers. This led to a polarization in the retail system between corporate, organizational customer relationships and consumer relationships. During the mid 1990s this large influx of private consumers coupled with an increased penetration of mobile telephones among large organizational buyers, private as well as public, had led to an increased polarization of customers and customer relations for suppliers, operators and retailers. From the early 1990s, there had been a sharp increase in the number of new customers and subscription sales. Towards the mid 1990s, there had been signs that both types of customers had become more active participants in the ongoing changes (e.g. more price-oriented and service-demanding private consumers and organizational buyers).

In addition to this customer polarization, there were also big differences in size between the different retailers. Figures for the early 1990s (1992) had indicated that only a small number of retailers (six) sold more than 1000 subscriptions per year, and more than 1700 retailers sold under 100 subscriptions per year. During the 1990s, all channel actors' attention had been directed from increased sales towards matters concerning diffusion of mobile telephony through new distribution channels, and towards internal channel efficiency, cost reductions and effectiveness.

CHANNEL ENTRY STRATEGIES – WHAT ARE THE ALTERNATIVES?

Reading through the report, Jan Olsen was able to draw two additional, important conclusions, apart from the polarization trend among customers which needed a strategic decision:

- A trend towards fewer and more intense supplier/operator–distributor contacts
- Increased internal network interdependencies and tensions

When comparing the general network and retailer orientations of the three major telephone suppliers and of the three operators over time, some strong similarities had emerged. All suppliers and operators had narrowed down the number of contacts with retailers, while simultaneously intensifying and centralizing remaining retailer contacts. The contacts had become more stable and structured.

The contacts between a smaller number of powerful actors had become more complex. The network positions and position changes of one company in the distribution system had become more dependent on the positions and position changes of others in the densely connected inter-organizational marketing network. The mobilization for change and coordination developed further as the marketing network became more tightly connected. Coordination and mobilization efforts had engaged more companies, moving towards more intense coordination and mobilization efforts between an operator, a telephone supplier and a large retail chain organization.

Reading through the analyses, Jan Olsen was left with four important, but difficult questions.

Questions

1. Which of the many ongoing structural channel changes was most important to consider when choosing channel entry strategy? What would be the short- and long-term implications of the rapid technological convergence between mobile telephone technology and information technology and media? What could one expect to be the channel structure consequences of this convergence?
2. Should the company go for the private consumers or the organizational buyers or both? What would be the strengths and weaknesses of each of these three options? How would it affect the choice of marketing channel choice?
3. How should Mobicom International enter the Swedish distribution network for mobile telephones? What alternative market entry

strategies are there to consider and what are the strengths and weaknesses of the different strategies? How could the general technological and organizational changes and the choice of customer focus affect the choice of channel strategy?

4. What additional information is needed in order to formulate market entry strategies for Mobicom in Sweden?

References and further reading

Andersson, P. and Mölleryd, B. (1998) Telecommunication services in context: distribution consequences of technological change and convergence. *International Journal of Service Industry Management*, 8(5): 453–473.

Andersson, P. and Mölleryd, B. (1999) Channel network change and behavioral consequences of network connectedness. *Journal of Business Research*, special issue on Relationship Marketing (forthcoming).

Stern, L.W., El-Ansary, A.I. and Coughlan, A.T. (1996) *Marketing Channels*, (5th edn). Englewood Cliffs, NJ: Prentice Hall International.

Webster, F.E. (1991) *Industrial Marketing Strategy*. Chapter 8. New York: John Wiley.

2

Ways of applying segmentation strategies: recession in the Hungarian beer market

József Berács

Case	Segmentation
Main focus	Domestic market, distribution, pricing, promotion
Subsidiary focus	Branding
Scene	Hungary
Players	Breweries, consumers
Product	Beer

Summary

The final decade of the twentieth century has seen dramatic changes both in economic structure and in consumer behaviour in Hungary. While the institutional system – the market economy – is mature and Hungary is preparing to join the European Union, real consumption per head of population was 5% lower in 1998 compared with 1988. Beer consumption alone has dropped by 35% in eight years and the trend shows as yet no sign of change.

The question for companies in the beer market is which marketing strategies can best strengthen the position of the individual companies. It seems likely that companies which use market segmentation methods are more capable of keeping their customers but this depends crucially on the existence of reliable market information.

© 2000 John Wiley & Sons, Ltd.
Understanding Marketing: A European Casebook edited by Celia Phillips, Ad Pruyn and Marie-Paule Kestemont.

Introduction

Product segmentation is the case area here, with an emphasis on the domestic market and branding. This and Case 14 both focus on beer. Case 2 looks at the challenges to a once thriving industry posed by a combination of rapid reorganization in the producing companies and a fall in consumer demand.

Domestic beer consumption in Hungary, like that in the Czech Republic, has fallen over the last ten years. But unlike in the Czech Republic, the fall has been dramatic even in the context of a depressed market for all consumer products. The case gives us the background on these changes in company structure and consumption and then concentrates on the potential offered by brand and consumer segmentation.

Beer consumption in Hungary rose throughout the 1980s, reaching a peak in 1990. Over this period Hungary ranked high among beer-consuming countries. By 1998, with beer consumption per head at about two-thirds (65%) of the 1990 figure, it was more comparable with the low-consumption countries. Unlike other countries which have suffered a drop in beer consumption, the complementary product appears to be soft drinks rather than wine.

This change has taken place against a backdrop of change in concentration and ownership of Hungarian brewery companies. By 1997 the ten main Hungarian breweries of the 1980s had become five – four owned by three European companies and the fifth (and that with the largest market share) by the South African company, SAB. The change in market shares over the 1990s is shown. There is also a group of licensed imported beers.

After this overview, we are shown alternative ways of segmenting the market. The first is by product type or price and trends here are presented. The second and main part of the case concentrates on segmentation by consumer. The main consumer groups and preferred beer outlets are discussed before findings on recent changes in consumer types are introduced.

One characteristic of Hungarian beer consumption is that people generally buy either domestic or foreign beer, and not both. The 1990s scenario has shown a slight rise both in consumer types who prefer domestic brands and in those who like foreign brands. Between them they accounted for over four-fifths (84%) of consumer types. Might this point the way to future expansions in the market?

The final section covers the advertising budgets of the main brands since 1996, when beer television advertising was made legal.

Questions focus on further possibilities of segmentation of product and consumer.

KEYWORDS

Beer, competition, declining market, changes in economic system, choice, loyalty, branding.

Case

BACKGROUND AND DEVELOPMENTS IN THE BEER MARKET

The president of the Association of Hungarian Breweries (MSSz) held a press conference on 8 May 1998. He described the market situation in the first quarter of that year: beer consumption had declined by 4.8% compared with the same period the year before despite the mild, springlike January and February. Even the experts did not know the reason for this fall. Only a year before, the decline had appeared to be slowing down, with a 1% decline in 1997 over 1996.

Back in 1990 average consumption per head had been 105 litres per year and this had accounted for 90% of the production of Hungarian breweries (11 million hectolitres). In addition, for several decades the industry had been carrying out a modernization programme in its breweries.

Data on beer consumption per head over the past ten years are given in Table 2.1. The fall in consumption from its peak in 1990 is clearly visible.

Table 2.2 puts these figures in context by giving beer consumption for some other European countries. The table shows two things. In the first place in 1991, Hungary was a high-consumption beer country, ranking with the United Kingdom, only a little behind Austria, Ireland and Denmark. Secondly, by 1997, although most countries have seen a decline, Hungary has fallen comparatively more – and compares with the lower beer consumption countries such as Spain and Sweden.

By 1997 the beer turnover had fallen to 7.1 million hectolitres and the seven main domestic factories were now in the hands of five foreign companies as a result of takeovers due in part to this drop in consumption.

A Mintel report describes a general Europe-wide decline in beer consumption of about 10% overall in the early 1990s. Reasons given vary from costs to country, and in some places reflect a rise in drinking

TABLE 2.1   Beer consumption per capita, per annum, Hungary, 1980–1998

Year	Beer consumption (litres per capita)
1980	86.0
1990	105.3
1991	101.1
1992	94.0
1993	83.9
1994	84.7
1995	75.3
1996	71.3
1997	70.0
1998	68.3

Source: *Statistical Yearbook of Hungary*, 1997.

TABLE 2.2   Beer consumption per capita in selected European countries, 1991 and 1997

Country	1991	1997
Austria	123.7	113.3
Czech Republic	No data available	160.0
Denmark	125.9	116.7
France	40.5	37.0
The Netherlands	90.5	86.4
Ireland	123.0	123.7
United Kingdom	109.0	103.6
Germany	No data available	131.1
Spain	71.0	67.0
Sweden	60.0	61.7

Source: HVG, 13 June 1998, p. 62; CMBC, 1998.

wine as an alternative to beer. While there has been little change in wine consumption, that of soft drinks and mineral water has risen substantially. Within the thirst-quenching drinks sector, beer's share of 58% in 1990 in Hungary had dropped to 34.5% in 1998.

The revenue of Hungarian beer companies fell in consequence. By 1998, their yearly revenue was 124 billion forints (roughly half a million Euros), of which 31 billion forints went on tax. Taxes and other deductions totalled 69% of their net income. However, in 1998 consumption tax (which plays an important role in government income) grew by only 6% – that is at a slower rate than estimated inflation – so companies did not raise their prices significantly at the beginning of 1999.

THE MARKET PLAYERS

As already stated there were, at the beginning of the decade, seven domestic breweries operating in different parts of Hungary. The government privatized all of them over the 1990s. As a result, the entire Hungarian beer industry is now in foreign ownership. Table 2.3 shows the details.

TABLE 2.3   The ownership of domestic breweries in Hungary, 1997

Company	Owner	Country
Dreher Sörgyárak Rt Kőbányai Sörgyár Kanizsa Sörgyár	South African Brewery (SAB)	South Africa
Borsodi Sörgyár Rt	Interbrew	Belgium
Brau Union Hungária Sörgyárak Rt Soproni Sörgyár Martfűi Sörgyár	Brau Union AG	Austria
Amstel Sörgyár Rt	Heineken	The Netherlands
Pécsi Sörfőzde Rt	Ottakringer-Weickheim	Austria

Source: AC Nielsen Retail Audit.

It can be seen that two large companies, SAB (the world's third biggest producer) and Austrian Brau Union AG, each bought two factories, which greatly increased concentration. In addition, in 1998 the Komarom Beer Factory was acquired by the world's second largest producer, Heineken, which is running it under the name Amstel Beer Factory. Interbrew, which bought Borsodi Beer Factory, became in the meantime the world's fourth largest beer-producing company as a result of its expansion in Canada. Finally, the fifth and smallest market player is the Pécs Beer Brewing Rt, which was bought by the Austrian Ottakringer.

These changes in ownership took place at the beginning of the 1990s, so market competition has been developing under foreign

direction but mainly with the cooperation of Hungarian management. In a gradually shrinking market the balance of power between
these breweries has altered over the last seven years. Table 2.4 shows
this trend.

TABLE 2.4   Market share (%) of domestic breweries, by volume 1991–1997

Company owner	1991	1992	1993	1994	1995	1996	1997	1998
Dreher	47.0	46.7	42.8	40.5	41.0	36.9	36.9	35.1
Borsodi	26.3	24.2	25.5	27.3	26.6	27.3	27.5	27.3
Brau Union	12.6	14.1	16.4	18.4	18.8	21.4	21.6	23.8
Amstel	3.6	4.1	5.2	5.9	6.6	7.3	7.1	7.0
Pécs	10.5	10.9	10.1	8.1	7.0	7.1	6.9	6.8
Total	100.0	100.0	100.0	100.0	100.0	100.0	100.0	100.0

Source: Association of Hungarian Breweries (MSSz); company reports.

The lead of SAB has lessened, although it is still in possession of
more than one-third of the market. Heineken, with the smallest
turnover, has, on the other hand, doubled its quota.
   In addition to these big beer factories small, "mini" breweries made
an appearance, supplying groups of customers – a small town or a
few restaurants (Kaltenberg Sörözö is an example of this). Their
market share in revenue terms is below 1% nationwide.

RECENT MARKET DEVELOPMENTS WITHIN THE MAIN COMPANIES

The three big domestic beer factories are roughly in the same
position regarding turnover. Their previous losses had been mainly
caused by modernization investments and they are beginning to
recoup the benefit of these (Table 2.5).

Dreher Beer Factories Co.

Dreher increased its net income by 20% between 1997 and 1998 to 20
billion forints. Its market share has remained at about 35% after a
slight fall in the early 1990s. It spent more on technical development
than its competitors in both 1997 and 1998. As expected from a
market leader, it also spent most on advertising: in 1998 about 1.5
billion forints. The company has recently changed its advertising

TABLE 2.5 Balance sheet data for domestic breweries, Hungary, 1997

Company	Net income (billion forint)	Profit after payment of tax (million forint)	Production (thousand hl)	Market share (%)
Amstel	2.7	80.6	513	7.1
Borsodi	14.6	1418.0	2000	27.7
Brau Union	14.0	807.0	1552	21.5
Dreher	15.7	625.1	2659	36.8
Pécsi	4.3	60.0	499	6.9
Total	53.8	2990.7	7223	100.0

Source: HVG, 13 June, 1998, p. 61; company reports.

agency. Previously Bates Saatchi & Saatchi created its advertisements but the 1999 summer campaign running under the slogan "Time works for us" was conducted by DDB Budapest.

Borsodi Beer Factory Co.

Hungary's second biggest beer factory increased its net income in 1998 by 18% to about 17.33 billion forints. The profit after payment of taxes reached 1.77 billion forints. Although the company experienced a slight market loss in 1977 (0.4%) the books showed spectacular improvement. The company wants to strengthen the distribution of Hungary's most sought after light beer, Borsodi Beer, which is already taking up more than 30% of its market segment. The company expects its licensed premium beers of Stella Artois and Holsten to show sales increases of 71% and 26% respectively.

The Borsodi Beer Factory was the first in Hungary to make use of beerhouses operating in a franchise system. The success of the Café Rolling Rock beerhouse, which opened its doors in 1997 as the first one in the world, persuaded the new Belgian marketing manager of the company to develop a franchise system around the Belgian Beer Café, which opened in 1998 in Miskolc, as the first one in East–Central Europe. Recently a fourth member of the Café Rolling Rock network opened at the Feneketlen Lake in Budapest. With another four new houses due to be opened by the end of 1999, this will bring the number of outlets to eight.

Brau Union Hungária Beer Factories Co.

Following an investment of more than 1.5 billion forints, a special bottling and packaging production line was inaugurated in July 1999 in the Martfü factory of the Brau Union. The area of finished goods' storage was also doubled, so that it is now capable of storing one week's production. The company's market share is estimated to be about 25% in 1999. Net income resulting from sales was 14.29 billion forints in 1998, exceeding the previous year's income by 280 million forints. After tax profit has doubled and reached 1.66 billion forints.

Amstel Beer Factory Co.

The company continued its previous market policy. Its conscious efforts at brand development seem to have been followed by the other three leading beer factories. This is clearly shown by the increase in the companies' advertising costs (Table 2.6) from 2410 million in 1997 to 4430 million forints in 1999, in which Amstel's share has lessened.

TABLE 2.6   Advertising costs of largest breweries based on list prices, Hungary (million forint)

Company	1998	1999, first quarter
Dreher	1567.2	103.8
Borsodi Beer Factory	1335.8	146.6
Brau Union	1043.9	74.3
Amstel	359.9	53.6
Pécsi Brewery	122.4	0.1
Total	4429.2	378.4

Source: Mediagnózis, 1999.

In the first quarter of 1999 Amstel again spent more than its competitors, especially when its share in turnover is taken into account. It strove to make use of various cultural events and connect the brand Amstel to them. Amstel was one of the major sponsors at the exhibition in the Buda Castle of the Masters of Folk Art, on 20 August, the day of the founding of the Hungarian state. It is the biggest event of its kind in Budapest both in terms of number of exhibitors and as a tourist attraction.

Pécsi Brewery Co.

This company typically specialized in regional market chains and began to enlarge its distributional system in 1998. It had its biggest turnover in the Budapest market, but lagged behind in the media nationwide.

THE WHOLE MARKET

The GFK Hungária Market Research Institute gives figures which are relevant to the whole market. Their survey among the population produced the following results: in the first quarter of 1999 3% more beer was consumed and 14% more money was spent on beer in Hungarian households than in the corresponding period in 1998. Beer prices went up by 9% on average. The retail price of one litre of beer went up from 147 forints in 1998 to 160 forints in the first quarter of 1999. The difference between prices of the cheapest and most expensive beer also increased significantly. This partly reflects the recent introduction of the more expensive beers and their subsequent scarcity value.

COMPETITION BETWEEN BRANDS

Both new traditional domestic brands (e.g. Köbányai Világos, Soproni Ászok), and beers produced by foreign licence (e.g. Tuborg, Holsten), had already appeared on the production platform in the 1980s. One of the tasks of the new brewery owners was to revive those old brands or to provide Hungary with a few of their own brands whether through imports or local production. Brands distributed by the individual companies according to categories "cheap" and "premium" are shown in Table 2.7.

If we only consider price as a segmenting factor, then – according to the Association of Hungarian Breweries (MSSz) – four categories of customers can be distinguished. Their share of the market has remained fairly stable over the last five years. They are shown in Table 2.8.

The prices of premium beers are at least 50–60% higher than those of cheap light beers. The market share of beers in middle categories

TABLE 2.7   Brands produced and distributed in Hungary

Company owner	Cheap	Premium/Special
Dreher Beer Factories Co.	Világos: Kőbányai/Világos Balatoni/Kanizsai Arany Ászok/Korona/Kinizsi	Dreher, Pils/Lager/Bak Hofbräu, Lager/Pils
Borsodi Beer Factory Co.	Borsodi: Világos/Rákóczi/ Kinizsi	Holsten, Pils/Premium Spaten, Rolling Rock, Stella Artois
Brau Union Hungária Beer Factories Co.	Soproni Ászok	Kaiser, Steffl, Gösser, Schwechater, Zipfer, Schlossgold
Amstel Beer Factory Co.	–	Amstel, Gold/Pils Kapsreiter, Talléros
Pécsi Brewery Co.	Szalon Beer	Gold Fassl, Glide

Source: HVG, company reports.

TABLE 2.8   Segmentation of the Hungarian beer
market, by volume

Categories	1992	1997
Cheap light beers	67.5	68.9
Medium category beers	8.6	3.8
Premium beers	23.2	25.2
Special beers	0.6	1.1
Total	100.0	100.0

Source: Association of Hungarian Breweries (MSSz), 1998.

has declined gradually while that for light beers has changed very little. Looking at products included in the category of special beers, such as the non-alcoholic Schlossgold, a very slight increase in turnover can be seen, but it is still low.

The range of brands in the premium category in 1995 was as follows:

Hofbräu	(7%)
Steffl	(12%)
Amstel	(15%)
Kaiser	(24%)
Dreher	(25%)
other	(17%)

Further details of segmentation are provided in Tables A2.1, A2.2 and A2.3.

CHARACTERISTICS OF BEER CONSUMERS

Apart from segmenting the beer itself, it is also important to segment the customer target. There are many varied consumers lying behind the fall in beer consumption. The market research company Marketing Centrum (1998) conducted a survey on consumer habits in October in 1995 and 1997. In 1995 only 36% of the people surveyed said they drank beer. In 1997, the figure was 41%. Clearly more people are drinking less beer. In fact, the main fall is in home consumption. In 1997 only 14% of people said they had beer in the home compared with 41% in 1995.

The restructuring of the hospitality business has made it more attractive to consume beer in restaurants and pubs. While beer turnover in the catering trade at the beginning of the decade was only 5.3% of total beer consumption, it had increased to around 20% by 1997.

In May 1998, Medián Public Opinion and Market Research Institute conducted a survey of 1500 people about their beer consumption and half of all adults said they drank beer, if only occasionally. Real beer consumers were defined as those who drank beer regularly at least once a week. These make up 19% of the population. Beer drinking is a "masculine" habit. Thirty-four per cent of men are regular beer consumers whereas only 5% of women fall in the same category. Three times as many middle-aged (30–49-year-olds) drink beer at least once a week compared with people over sixty. Higher school leaving certificates and higher salaries also make one more likely to be a beer consumer. There are no regional or urban/rural differences in beer consumption. This survey also found that people were three times more likely to drink beer in the home rather than elsewhere.

There are two different "worlds of taste" amongst consumers. The first group prefer the traditional domestic brands; the second shows a preference for "look alikes" of foreign brands. This is quite marked. Thirty-four per cent of consumers only drink domestic beer, 20% licensed beers (of which Dreher is one). Detailed figures are given in Table A2.4.

These habits seem to be a result of cultural rather than material factors. Licensed brands are mostly consumed by intellectuals, those enjoying higher pay or those living in the capital. Domestic brands are preferred by village people, and those with lower education and salary. The young also prefer licensed beers. Within these differences brand loyalty is strong. Nearly three-quarters (74%) of beer drinkers have drunk the same brand for two to three years.

TABLE 2.9   Changes in consumer figures. Hungary 1990, 1994, 1998 (percentages)

Consumer types	Relevance of marketing	Distribution		
		1990	1994	1998
Resigned poor	Domestic brand is preferred	15	25	40
Struggling poor	They do not have strong preferences	8	9	7
Mainstreamers	Domestic brands are popular	35	25	22
Aspirers	Entranced by foreign brands	6	11	17
Successful	The group most sensitive to Western brands and high quality products	14	11	5
Unique	Only their preferences matter	6	10	2
Reformers	Quality products	10	10	6

Source: Young and Rubicam (1990, 1994); Budapest University of Economic Sciences (BUES) Marketing Department (1998).

A breakdown of consumer types is given in Table 2.9. It is clear from this table that the main change has been in that group which prefer home brands – the "resigned poor". To some extent the rise in this group is offset by the fall in "mainstreams". Taking these groups together, however, we see an overall rise – from 50% in 1990 to 62% in 1998. Change in those enthusiastic about foreign ("aspirers" and "the successful") beer has also been positive – but only slightly so – from 20% in 1990 to 22% in 1998. None of this explains the actual fall in beer consumption!

OTHER MARKETING FACTORS

Before 1997, the advertising of all alcoholic products in the media was prohibited. The main marketing tools used by companies had to depend on price manipulation and the definition of the distribution channel. The expansion of choice in products in the 1990s could not be accompanied by powerful advertising campaigns and so has not resulted in strong loyalty for brands.

In 1997 the advertising of alcohol on television became legal. (This did not include spirits which may still not be advertised on radio or television.) The effects are still to be seen. It is felt that non-alcoholic beer (which *was* advertised earlier) had not benefited from its possibilities. Soft drinks, however, which were aggressively advertised over the period, have boomed. Table A2.5 shows the amount of money spent on advertising and the number of advertising spots from 1996 to 1999. It shows in particular the consistently big effort made over the period to promote Dreher, Holsten and Borsodi.

Questions

Aiming at better understanding of the market.

1. What segmentation basis might be useful in segmenting the Hungarian beer market?
2. What data on consumers would you need in order to select the best method of segmentation and decide on segments to be targeted?
3. Design a short questionnaire (eight to ten questions plus classification questions) which a beer company could use to obtain this data.
4. The case shows a current trend away from home beer consumption. What factors may be relevant in determining the future balance between home and out-of-home consumption?
5. What potential can you see for increasing the consumption of quality (premium) beers?

References and further reading

Acs, F. and Meiszterics, E. (1998) Többen isznak kevesebb sört (More drink less beer). *Kreativ Kutatás* Vol. 1, No. 1, 14 pp.
Élelmiszer (1999) Ahol a vásárlók többnyire azonos márkát vesznek,

Növekvő márkatudatosság. (Where customers purchase more or less the same brands. Increasing brand awareness). July, pp. 34–36.

Élelmiszer (1999) Mit üzen a sörreklám a bolti eladáshoz? Nők veszik, férfiak isszák. (What can we learn from beer advertisements for retail sale? Ladies buy, men drink). July, pp. 48–51.

Figyelő (1999) Rátöltenek (They are topping up), Brau Union. July 15–21, p. 15.

Hoohey, J.G. et al. (1998) *Marketing Strategy and Competitive Positioning* (2nd edn). Hemel Hempstead: Prentice Hall Europe.

Horváth, G. (1998) Rosszul kezdte az idei évet a söripar (The brewery industry has had a bad start this year). *Magyar Hirlap* May 9, p. 10.

HVG (1998) Sörállás (Beer situation). *Heti Vilag Gazdesag (HVG)* June, pp. 13, 61–74.

Kucsera, Á. (1999) A magyar sörpiac marketing-elemzése (Marketing analysis of the Hungarian beer market). *Diplomamunka*, April 1999. Thesis work.

László, A. (1998) Erről jut eszembe (By the way). *Sörlevél* No. 3, January, Newsletter of Brau Union Hungária Sörgyárak Rt.

Papp, Z. (1998) Események a söriparban (Events in the beer industry). *KREATIV* Vol. VII, No. 5, May, p. 49.

Szentesi, M. (1998) A fogyasztói márkahűség jelentősége a hazai söripari marketingben (The importance of consumer brand loyalty in the domestic beer market). Thesis work, BUES Postgraduate Studies.

Appendix

TABLE A2.1   Nielsen's seven segments in beer retail

Segment types	Distribution of turnover (%)		
	1996	1997	1998
Standard light	65.8	64.8	66.3
Premium light	4.1	3.0	2.5
Dreher	8.6	8.8	8.7
Licence	17.8	19.5	18.5
Imported	1.1	0.9	0.8
Alcohol-free	2.0	2.5	2.6
Other	0.6	0.4	0.5
Total	100.0	100.0	100.0

Source: AC Nielsen Retail Audit.

TABLE A2.2   Characteristics of standard light/of cheap category/ segment brands in the retailing sector. By share in sales and price

Brand	Share in the sales of the segment		Average price per litre (forint)	
	1997	1998	1997	1998
Borsodi Világos*	[1]	[1]	133	151
Kőbányai Világos*	[2]	[4]	126	141
Arany Ászok	[3]	[2]	136	155
Soproni Világos*	[4]	[3]	132	151
Pécsi Szalon	[5]	[5]	129	146
Kanizsai Világos*	[6]	[6]	126	137
Total	89.7%	90.5%	No data available	No data available

* "Világos" refers to a rough "village" beer type.

Source: AC Nielsen Retail Audit.

TABLE A2.3   Characteristics of licence (of premium category) and
Dreher Pils brands in the retailing sector, by share in sales and price

Licence brand	Share in the sales of the segment		Average price per litre (forint)	
	1997	1998	1997	1998
Kaiser Prémium	[1]	[1]	191	208
Amstel	[2]	[2]	199	217
Steffl	[3]	[3]	181	201
Holfbräu	[4]	[4]	181	202
Gösser	[5]	[5]	194	218
Holsten	[6]	[6]	193	215
Stella Artois	[8]	[7]	211	231
Gold Fassl	[10]	[8]	190	191
Spaten	[7]	[9]	178	203
Rolling Rock	[9]	[10]	213	228
Tuborg	[11]	[11]	225	231
Total	91.2%	94.8%	No data available	No data available
Dreher Pils	[1]	[1]	175	196

Source: AC Nielsen Retail Audit.

TABLE A2.4   Favourite new brands

Brand	Favourite	Second choice	Consumes occasionally	Never drinks it
Borsodi Világos*	21	11	15	53
Arany Ászok	13	12	16	59
Amstel	13	8	16	63
Kőbányai Világos*	10	12	13	65
Soproni Ászok	8	9	20	63
Dreher	8	8	20	64
Kaiser	7	9	15	69
Gösser	3	4	10	83
Steffl	2	4	14	80
Holsten	1	1	14	84
Egyéb	17	20	21	42

* "Világos" refers to a cheaper beer (see Table A2.2).

Source: HVG, June 1998.

TABLE A2.5

(a) Television advertising for beer, Hungary 1996–1999

	1996	1997	1998	1999
Number of spots	6.121	133.074	18.610	37.805
Total cost/thousand forint	935.617	2278.625	4062.993	7277.234

(b) Leading brands (percentage of total sales by volume)

	1996	%		1997	%		1998	%		1999	%
1.	Borsodi	18.88	1.	Dreher	16.26	1.	Arany Ászok	13.20	1.	Dreher	12.76
2.	Amstel	18.35	2.	Kaiser	10.53	2.	Dreher	12.33	2.	Holsten	10.85
3.	Rolling Rock	17.59	3.	Kőbányai Világos	10.25	3.	Holsten	11.73	3.	Borsodi	10.47
4.	Holsten	14.71	4.	Borsodi	9.12	4.	Borsodi	9.28	4.	Arany Ászok	9.23
5.	Dreher	6.15	5.	Amstel	8.80	5.	Stella Artois	8.13	5.	Amstel	8.28
6.	Kőbányai Világos	5.76	6.	Holsten	7.71	6.	Steffl	7.20	6.	Stella Artois	6.80
7.	HB	4.83	7.	Stella Artois	7.23	7.	Soproni	9.93	7.	Kaiser	6.44
8.	Steffl	3.10	8.	Gösser	5.07	8.	HB	6.48	8.	HB	5.60
9.	Arany Ászok	2.47	9.	Arany Ászok	4.92	9.	Amstel	5.67	9.	Rolling Rock	5.43
10.	Kaiser	2.29	10.	Rolling Rock	4.80	10.	Kaiser	5.10	10.	Steffl	4.73

Note: The TV advertisements show the efforts companies are making to develop brands. Costs calculated on the basis of list prices could in reality be smaller due to discounts given to important clients; other advertising which might be important in the beer industry could include the sponsorship of special events such as beer festivals.

Source: AC Nielsen Media Survey.

3

MD Foods amba: a new world of sales and marketing

Mogens Bjerre

Case	Business to business
Main focus	Sales and marketing organization
Subsidiary focus	Branding
Scene	Denmark, Europe-wide
Players	Manufacturer, retailing outlets
Product	Dairy products

Summary

A special feature of the dairy industry is the continuous flow of the raw material, milk, which keeps flowing regardless of the sales. The specific milk products to be developed have to be decided at a point when customer targets are not fully known. This puts considerable pressure on the sales organization to identify product and customer priorities. The value of the milk is increased by producing butter, cheese, yoghurt or milk powder and branding them.

Few international brands have been introduced to the dairy industry, dominated as it is by national brands, though generics (such as Brie, feta and Emmental) are sold in considerable volume. Another major method of profit maximization has arisen through MD's introduction of the idea of key account managers for linking production to key retailing outlets.

This case concentrates on the reorganization of MD over the 1990s in order to take advantage of changes in the market for milk products in Europe.

© 2000 John Wiley & Sons, Ltd.
Understanding Marketing: A European Casebook edited by Celia Phillips,
Ad Pruyn and Marie-Paule Kestemont.

Introduction

This is one of two cases which have a business-to-business context from the point of view of sales and marketing organizations. Readers are introduced to a well-established Danish dairy cooperative, the fourth largest in Europe and with a few, well-known Europe-wide brands. Over the past few years it has combined with Arla in product development, sales and marketing in Sweden and Finland. Sales are "business to business" – customers are retail chains in many countries, but particularly Europe.

Readers are introduced to the detailed background and the changes in markets over the past few years Europe-wide are discussed. The withdrawal of EU subsidies to the export of dairy products to non-EU countries in 1996 has had a major effect on the direction of marketing effort, as has the increasing centralization of food retail, both in terms of the reduction in its number of retail organizations dealing in food, and their increasing centralization in product mix planning. MD's strategy for dealing with such pressures is described – from the first pilot in 1992–1997, up to the future plans for business unit managers dealing with MD product management throughout Europe.

This case invites readers to consider these strategies and their strengths and weaknesses when dealing with these kinds of products. This is a useful chance to study the mechanics of sales and marketing organizations in different business-to-business environments.

KEYWORDS

Dairy industry, branding, labels, regional retailers, account management, trade marketing.

Case

Changing the organization and structures in sales and marketing may be initiated for different reasons. The reasons presented in this case arise from the necessity to adjust organizations and structures in response to changes among customers and in accordance with the strategies they pursue. Thus, the introduction and development of key account management and trade marketing in MD Foods amba are the focus of this case.

MD Foods amba$^{(MD)}$ is a dairy cooperative. In 1998 it was estimated that it was owned by 8728 Danish farmers (**www.mdfoods. dk**). MD's headquarters are situated in Århus, Denmark, and production facilities are spread throughout the country. Sales subsidiaries have been established in England, France, Germany, Greece, Italy, Norway, Poland, Sweden, in the USA and Canada, and in the Middle East.

The company was formally established in 1970 and results from a number of mergers and acquisitions in the Danish dairy industry over the past 20 years. As a result MD has become by far the largest dairy in Denmark. It is now the fourth largest dairy in Europe, in terms of tonnes of milk accepted for production (Børsen, 1998). The company is based on cows' milk as its major raw material ingredient and produces milk, milk powder, yoghurt, and different kinds of cheese.

Through MD Foods International (MDI), MD has established its own production and distribution facilities in the English market. In addition, MD has developed a cooperative with Arla in Sweden (the counterpart of MD in Sweden) under the name Scandairy K/S markets. This cooperation between MD and Arla aims to enhance product development, sales, and marketing of speciality products in the Scandinavian markets and enables MD and Arla to compete in the European market as a whole. MD and Arla have also developed further cooperation as Arla's sales force in the Finnish market handles MD's products in addition to its own. MD and Arla have divided sales and marketing tasks between them. MD is handling its own key account contacts and Arla is handling operational sales tasks in the relevant retailers' stores.

INDUSTRY BACKGROUND – EUROPE

The dairy industry in Europe is dominated by national firms, which primarily serve the market from which they originate. Most of these firms produce generic products, although some geographical differences may be identified. In some markets yellow cheese is dominant, in some white cheese leads, and in yet others milk is the staple.

A special feature of the dairy industry is the continuous flow of raw material – milk – which keeps flowing in the short term no matter how the sales are. The use of milk must be prioritized at a point in time when the customers are not known, and this puts considerable pressure on the sales organization to be able to identify product and customer priorities. The value of the milk can be increased by the production of butter, cheese, yoghurt and milk powder, all of which are preferably branded.

Few international brands have been introduced in the dairy industry as it is dominated by national brands (Kraft's Philadelphia is an example). However, a considerable volume is sold as generics, marketed by type, such as Brie, feta, Emmental etc., and internationally known. In other words, MD faces not only national and local producers of generic products but also the international brands produced by large international producers, typically with strong and long experience in developing and maintaining brands.

The dairy sector has been in a highly competitive situation for some time and in particular since 1996 when the European Union decided to end export subsidies to non-EU countries in relation to dairy products – primarily feta cheese sold to the Middle East. As MD accounted for approximately one-third of the total EU exports of feta cheese, this development has put especially heavy pressure on MD to convert the milk used for feta production to other products for sale within the EU and mainly to existing customers. MD and its competitors thus had to switch their production of feta cheese either to milk powder or yellow cheese. However, these two product groups provide a limited profit, because they are sold as commodities.

Another factor to take into account is the concentration among retailers in Europe. This is high, especially in the north – Germany, Benelux, UK and Scandinavia. On average the top five retailers account for more than 75% of the total turnover in fast moving consumer goods (FMCG). The organization of retailers' buying function has also changed and has become more centralized, so that the buyer is the decision-maker, often without any interference from other functions in the retailer's organization.

COMPANY BACKGROUND AND DEVELOPMENT

MD has traditionally been a product-oriented company. Given a fairly constant supply of milk, its preoccupation has to be which product group to develop at any particular time.

MD also faces very different market situations in the different countries, ranging from a very dominant position in all relevant product categories (Denmark) to a niche position in a few categories (Sweden). It is therefore not sensible to implement an identical marketing structure in each market: local conditions and MD's position in local markets must always be the first consideration.

In addition, branding has been local to each market with a few exceptions (Lurpak butter, Buko cheese and Finello shredded cheese are examples of the few international brands produced by MD). A further branding complication lies in the fact that MD produces private brand labels for some leading retailers throughout Europe: a product sold as a brand in one national market may feature as a private label in another.

KEY ACCOUNT MANAGEMENT AND TRADE MARKETING EVOLUTION – THE INFLUENCE OF LARGE RETAILERS

A particular large international retailer has initiated the evolution of key account management. Analyses showed that this one customer's total purchase, in terms of the retailer's European turnover from MD, was higher than the turnover of many of MD's subsidiaries; in other words, key customers can be as important as geographical markets.

This retailer had centralized its buying function to improve buying conditions and was stocking its stores with identical MD products. In this way, adaptations to local markets were minimized.

As MD's sales organization was based purely on geographical and national considerations, strongly supported by the need for local language skills, the retailer in question forced MD to respond differently and to decide how to cope with the conflict between the customer and internal structures in sales and marketing.

Until 1990 MD's sales and marketing organization had traditionally focused on individual stores rather than on retail chains or key accounts. This was based on the notion that most decisions regarding assortment, pricing, activities and so on were made at the retail store level, not at central retailer level.

After this, with the introduction of ideas of key account management as described, came recognition from MD that there was a need to analyse sales in different ways. An internal project was set up in which the concept and potential of key account management was to be examined in detail. This introduction of key account management and trade marketing was based on a number of central expectations about retail development in the run up to the millennium.

- Twenty retail groups/buying organizations will represent 80% of total FMCG turnover
- Many strong regional retailers will develop
- Retailers will increasingly make decisions at a central rather than local level
- Consumer access to manufacturers will be through retail stores

As the Danish market has high retailer concentration and MD has such a high market share in the dairy category, the Danish brand of MD was chosen to pilot the introduction of key account management in its sales and marketing organization.

The marketing department was divided into two areas, one working with consumer marketing (product and brand management) and one working with trade marketing (in-store marketing and space management).

Three key account managers and three trade managers were appointed in 1990, and were supposed to work as teams related to the specific key accounts served by the key account manager. The three key account managers referred to the Danish sales director and the trade managers referred to a national trade marketing manager located in the marketing department.

The two organizations were located at Vejle (sales) and Århus (marketing) about 70 kilometres away from each other. Figure 3.1 shows the structure described.

The levels of the positions illustrated in Figure 3.1 are not indications of levels of seniority but show that the trade managers are coordinated by a trade marketing manager, while the coordination of the key account managers is handled by the sales director. It should be noted that coordination within trade marketing focuses on utilization of know-how, while coordination within sales focuses on optimization of the sales force.

The main changes lay in the introduction of this "one entrance to MD's organization" and it was partly based on an expectation that

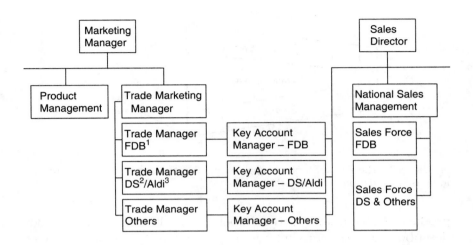

FIGURE 3.1   MD Foods: relation between key account management and trade marketing, Denmark, 1990. FDB, "Fællesforeningen for Danske Brugsforeninger" (the Danish Co-op). DS, Dansk Supermarked, a privately held retail group. Aldi is the Danish subsidiary of the German retail group of that name. Source: in-house material provided by MD.

retailers would organize similarly, i.e. that the buyers would gradually take over more responsibilities. Furthermore the key account manager was seen as a "spearhead" pinpointed at the key account representing the whole organization. This is shown in Figure 3.2.

Coordination of key account managers' efforts was handled in two ways, depending on the effect on the overall strategies for MD. Effects on general sales and marketing strategies were coordinated by the sales director, whereas operational effects were objects for negotiation between the key account manager and the functions involved. For example, need for in-store activities in a specific retail chain had to be negotiated with the sales manager as it could conflict with brand management interests or interests within the sales organization.

MD was convinced that the key account management system would be the competitive edge that would ensure the continuous development of customer relations. In view of the increasing customer focus on own brands, MD developed an internal priority list related to sales of MD branded products, private labels and generic

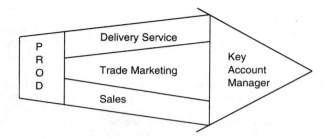

FIGURE 3.2   The key account manager as spearhead, Denmark, 1990. Source: in-house material provided by MD Foods, 1990.

products. (Own brands, private labels, house brands etc. are used to describe the customer's interest in exclusivity for certain products and/or product names/trademarks.) The priority is as follows, in descending order of importance:

- MD brands in speciality cheeses
- MD brands in other cheeses
- Private brands
- Generic products

It is important to recall that the overall objective of the sales and marketing department is to create the highest possible value from the continuous flow of raw materials.

MD has made presentations on its work. Marketing is defined as:

- A philosophy of starting from the customer's position and possible developments
- A way of developing customized solutions
- A way of adapting the organization to deliver these solutions in the context of time, quality and costs
- A way of monitoring marketing and financial issues at customer level

Key account management is defined as a tool to implement the following aspects of trade marketing:

- The use of a dedicated salesman as key account manager for each trade customer
- The planning and monitoring of systems with each trade customer
- The agreement of terms which manage costs and profits at a desired level
- The development of direct product profitability tools in order to establish and strengthen dialogue with the trade customer

REFINING THE SYSTEM (1991–1997)

This period saw a refinement of the system described above, and has brought about no fundamental changes. Initially the new concepts were tested in the Danish market, and the plan was then gradually to apply these concepts in other markets.

Although new people were employed as key account managers and trade marketing managers as the original post-holders moved to other positions, these changes did not affect the organization of MD or its relation to the key accounts. Only one minor change was introduced: the profile of personal characteristics has been introduced to aid the process of appointing key account managers in order to ensure the best possible match between key account and trade account managers. Training is also important. New key account managers have been generally recruited externally, and are expected "to be able to handle the profession as they arrive in MD" as Jens Refslund of MD Foods puts it. Because of this the development of in-house training began to be seen as a key issue. The set-up is in principle identical for all key accounts, providing all key account managers with the same possibilities of back-up.

A further change in organization was brought about by the steady increase in workload experienced by key account managers over the period. Adjustments had to be made within the organization to allow for this.

Over the period 1992 to 1994 the organizational principles of the Danish pilot were implemented in Sweden. Initial reactions from major Swedish retailers were negative: at MD's organization there they could see no reason for doing business with a key account manager. One such retailer said "A key account manager would not be able to handle negotiations and meetings at a retail group level, at the regional levels and at the same time follow-up in the stores!" (Jens Refslund). Further developments have been confined to Denmark.

1998 – THE NEXT STEP

It was decided that MD should increase the number of key account managers from three to four over 1998. At the same time the key account managers were to take on staff responsibility for the sales force dedicated to "their" key account; i.e., the sales force aimed at "Fællesforeningen for Danske Brugsforeninger" (FDB) does not serve stores belonging to other key accounts. As the sales forces of two of the key account managers are combined, MD operates three national sales forces. These three sales forces vary considerably in size (the largest consists of 15 people, the smallest of only four) and vary considerably in relation to the tasks they handle. A large sales force serves a retailer with autonomous store managers. It deals with tasks such as sales, merchandising, placing signs and posters, introducing new campaigns, deciding on location for displays etc. A small sales force will serve a highly centralised retailer and the tasks handled will fall primarily in merchandising, establishing displays, and the like.

This new structure is based on an analysis of the key account, their strategy and past cooperation. Therefore the management style, culture, and strategy of the key account are all important in relation to the structure and strategy MD will develop.

At the same time the title "national key account manager" was changed to "business unit manager" with responsibilities equivalent to those of the sales director. This is an important new development within MD, as the sales and marketing effort to a key account is considered to be as important as the sales and marketing effort towards the geographic market. Simultaneously different organizational structures emerge in sales and marketing, as the need for different organizational responses are recognized at key account level. Therefore, one business unit manager is supported by a "key account manager" to handle the workload. The structure supporting the sales and marketing effort towards one retailer may be quite different from the structure supporting the sales and marketing efforts towards another retailer. The differences are related to the different structures of the two retailers and to the difference in volume they represent vis-à-vis MD.

Internal career development and the gradual development of specific own competencies in relation to key accounts have also been introduced as part of the new organizational set-up. This implies that the development of a business unit manager takes time and needs careful planning and timing. The new organizational structure is illustrated in Figure 3.3, which is only concerned with sales.

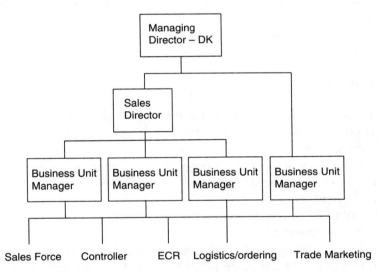

FIGURE 3.3   MD Foods' business unit manager structure and support functions, Denmark, 1998. Source: in-house material provided by MD Foods, 1998.

The lines in Figure 3.3 indicate that there are dedicated resources in other departments, focusing on the specific key accounts on an ad hoc basis. MD has already prepared the future organizational structure supporting the business unit manager. The structure has been implemented in the English market and MD expects that the structure will apply to the rest of Europe within the next two to three years.

FUTURE DEVELOPMENTS

MD has just recently been through the design process for the next "generation" of key account management and trade marketing in the Danish market. This is not expected to be applied in other markets – at this stage. However, internal exchange of experiences with specific solutions are to be intensified and MD's ambition is to develop a more coherent system over the coming years.

The new organization will be key-account focused and will transform all key account managers into business unit managers. Business unit refers to the business with the key account and the management of the team supporting this business relation. The relation between the two organizations is gradually becoming unique and closed in relation to the external environment.

Questions

1. Can you identify and argue for one organizational structure that would be able to handle MD Foods' challenge vis-à-vis key accounts?
2. If a key account were considered as important as a geographical market, how would you organize the sales and marketing department?
3. Describe the development for MD Foods in terms of internal need for coordination and planning.
4. What considerations do MD Foods need to take into account in formulating (a) their strategy for MD Foods brands in Europe? (b) their strategy for supplying own label brands in Europe?

References and further reading

Bjerre, M. (1999) The four types of key account management. PhD dissertation, Copenhagen Business School.
Børsen (Danish financial newspaper) (1998) MD Foods among Europe's top dairies. 19 January.
McDonald, M. and Rogers, B. (1998) *Key Account Management*. Oxford: Butterworth-Heinemann.

Millmann, A.F. and Wilson, K.J. (1995) Key Account Selling to Key Account Management. 10th Annual Conference on Industrial Marketing and Purchasing, University of Groningen, Netherlands.

Nielsen, A.C. (1995) *Europe Retail Trends*, Volume I.

Refslund, J. (1998) Interview by Mogens Bjerre, 17 September 1998.

4

Developing an international communication strategy for a brand: the NIVEA case

Marc Brenneiser and Richard Köhler

Case	Branding
Main focus	Global brand
Subsidiary focus	Brand awareness, international markets, advertising
Scene	Worldwide
Players	Beiersdorf, trademark rights, product
Product	Cosmetics

Summary

In the past quarter century, the NIVEA brand of Beiersdorf AG has developed from a skin cream to the world's largest brand for many skin- and body-care products. The legal prerequisites are now established which enable the marketing of NIVEA as a global brand. Up to now advertising campaigns have aimed to keep local characteristics. How should the company proceed if it wants to develop a uniform communication strategy for NIVEA? The company is faced with the task of planning a brand approach that caters for the altered market demands of the 1990s and development a *uniform communication strategy* for the NIVEA brand.

© 2000 John Wiley & Sons, Ltd.
Understanding Marketing: A European Casebook edited by Celia Phillips,
Ad Pruyn and Marie-Paule Kestemont.

Introduction

The emphasis of this case is firmly on a cosmetic product, and the NIVEA brand. This is one of two cases which deal with it. The focus here is on NIVEA as a global product. Since the 1950s, NIVEA has been trying to re-establish itself in this way after a period when it had been marketed through more than 30 foreign subsidiaries. To this end, over a forty-year period Beiersdorf AG has reacquired its trademark rights.

At the same time, the diversification of the NIVEA product to include more than the original and well-known NIVEA *Creme* carries problems of communication and recognition. The authors carefully describe studies on brand profile so that readers can think about how they would design advertisements which communicate NIVEA products. While main interest lies in the question of whether it is wise or practicable to devise a global advertising campaign for this product, and the kinds of advertising which would be most productive, a strong feature of the case is its discussion of customer segmentation in terms of the socio-cultural values of consumers.

KEYWORDS

Branding strategies (e.g. line extensions), international and global brands, international communication strategy (e.g. standardization and differentiation), international brand policy.

Case

The Hamburg-based company Beiersdorf AG employs some 17 000 people and has three divisions, each responsible for a number of brands: *Cosmed* handles brands such as NIVEA, 8x4, Atrix and Labello; *Medical* is responsible for brands such as Hansaplast and Eucerin. The third division is *Tesa*. Of these brands, NIVEA has the highest turnover and accounted for approximately 29.8% of the company's overall turnover by value in 1992. Figure 4.1 gives turn-over figures for NIVEA.

NIVEA *Creme* was introduced in 1911 in a yellow tin as the first stable greasing and moisturizing cream in the world. After serious declines in sales, the packaging design was replaced in 1925 with a

Turnover in DM millions

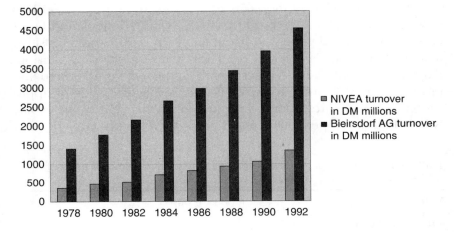

FIGURE 4.1 Development of turnover of the NIVEA brand and Beiersdorf AG.
Source: Beiersdorf AG.

considerably more striking visual design: the blue tin with the white
NIVEA livery. The communication concept was also revised at this
time. The brand was distinguished by the same unique selling
proposition that is still valid today: "mild, soothing and high-quality
body care for the whole family". The cream logo made its debut on
the NIVEA tin in 1959, with the word *Creme* being written in the
hand-written style characteristic for NIVEA. Figure 4.2 shows the
well-known product.

FIGURE 4.2 NIVEA *Creme*, the standard product. Source: Beiersdorf AG.

The range of products marketed under the NIVEA brand was expanded somewhat in the years after its initial launch. The 1970s saw many new skin-care products such as body lotions and facial cleanser introduced under the brand name. In the 1980s the positive image of NIVEA *Creme* was used for a major brand expansion. Existing products were replaced with improved versions and the product groups formed according to the respective fields of application (e.g. hair-care products) expanded. By the start of the 1990s, NIVEA had developed into a brand name for an entire array of skin-

TABLE 4.1   Overview of the most important new product launches under the NIVEA brand, Germany, 1911–1991

Year	Product	Product group
1911	NIVEA *Crème* for skin care	NIVEA *Creme* Internationally uniform under NIVEA *Creme* since 1959, without further product explanations
1930	NIVEA *Öl*	NIVEA *Sonne* (sun protection) Internationally uniform under NIVEA sun since 1991
1931	NIVEA *Schampu* (Shampoo)	NIVEA Haar (hair-care products) Internationally uniform under NIVEA Hair Care since 1991
1963	NIVEA body milk	NIVEA Milk (skin-care products) Internationally uniform under NIVEA body since 1990
1966	NIVEA Baby	NIVEA Baby (baby-care products) Internationally uniform designation since launch
1976	NIVEA *Creme Bad*	NIVEA *Bad* Internationally uniform under NIVEA Bath Care since 1996
1980	NIVEA After Shave Balsam	NIVEA Rasur (men's grooming products) Internationally uniform under NIVEA for Men since 1986
1982	NIVEA *Gesicht*	NIVEA *Gesicht* (facial care products) Marketed under the name NIVEA Visage since 1960 in France and since 1972 in Belgium
1991	NIVEA *Deo*	NIVEA *Deo* Internationally uniform designation since launch

Source: Beiersdorf AG.

TABLE 4.2   Reacquisition of NIVEA trademark rights 1952–1992

Year	Country
1952	The Netherlands
1956	Switzerland
1958	Argentina, Brazil
1963	Mexico
1966	Denmark
1968	Finland, African Commonwealth States (excluding South Africa)
1973	USA
1974	France
1977	Hong Kong, Thailand, Malaysia, Singapore, Gibraltar, Cyprus, Malta, Bermuda, The Bahamas, Jamaica, Barbados, Trinidad
1985	Norway
1992	Canada, South Africa, New Zealand, India, Pakistan, Israel, Australia, Great Britain, Ireland

Source: Beiersdorf AG.

and body-care products. Table 4.1 shows this process. It provides an overview of the most important new product launches under the brand name NIVEA in Germany (including changes in the respective product group designations).

The expansion of the product range was also able to take place on an international level on account of the increasing repurchase of foreign trademark rights (Table 4.2). Beiersdorf already had 14 foreign subsidiaries throughout the world in 1932, although the company only retained the trademark rights for Germany and Austria following the Second World War.

The repurchase at the end of 1992 of the foreign trademark rights (with the exception of Poland) also established the legal pre-requisites for marketing the world's largest brand for skin- and body-care products – now represented in more than 150 countries – as a global brand.

However, in view of the host of line extensions, the brand maintenance of NIVEA is a constant endeavour to strike the right balance between individual product interests and the necessity of finely-tuned branding of the entire NIVEA range. On the one hand, the NIVEA product line calls for the colours and shapes of the product designs to be coordinated while, on the other hand, the respective products also have to be oriented to competitor products in the context of a specific competitive situation.

In German consumer markets, NIVEA holds a superior position in numerous submarkets. It is the market leader for skin creams, lotions and deodorants. NIVEA also maintains a strong position in many other countries, and has even achieved market dominance in some.

In the past, an independent brand personality was established for each product group, i.e. every product group (e.g. facial care or hair-care) was based on an autonomous concept and had its very own brand image. (An independent brand personality was not immediately established for all products or product groups upon their launch. NIVEA Sonne, for example, was not developed as an independent product group until the start of the 1970s.) Furthermore, each product group was run as a profit centre and had its own marketing budget, own advertising campaigns and a special product benefit ("uniqueness"). Peculiarities in the respective submarkets, such as special consumer groups and individual profiles in the different countries, were taken into account by appropriate orientation of the advertising campaigns in the respective submarkets.

A major problem stems from the fact that trademark rights had been in third-party hands for a long time in numerous countries and no uniform principles or guidelines existed for global branding. This frequently resulted in different product ranges being available in different countries, replete with different product images and designations (e.g. NIVEA Sonne was marketed under the designation NIVEA Solaire in France and NIVEA sun in England). In order to imbue the products with a "local character", they have, among other things, been introduced in several countries in the appropriate local language and idiom and with advertising campaigns developed especially for these submarkets.

The values of the NIVEA brand can be characterized in the form of *fundamental values*, such as trust, sympathy and honesty, *competence values*, such as safety, mildness, naturalness and caring, as well as *pragmatic values*, such as timelessness, simplicity, overall availability and price credibility.

As a rule, every NIVEA product is positioned as mild and caring (brand core), although this has not always been taken into account in the past (the shaving products, for example, initially lacked a "care" component and, consequently, close proximity to the brand core; *see*

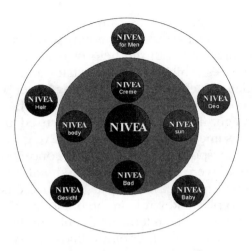

FIGURE 4.3   Brand profile of the NIVEA brand at the start of 1992

Figure 4.3). Furthermore, the product groups should be positioned in their submarkets as particularly caring and mild versions in comparison with competitor products.

In order to implement this brand strategy, regular studies concerning the *brand profile* have been conducted by means of consumer interviews. These studies showed that the brand profile constantly changes in the eye of the consumer. Figure 4.3 readily illustrates that the product groups NIVEA *Creme*, NIVEA sun, NIVEA body and NIVEA Bad have close proximity to the brand core from the consumer standpoint in the year 1992.

A fundamental aspect of the communication policy for NIVEA is that every advertising measure for a NIVEA product should, at the same time, always contribute to updating and reinforcing the image of all other NIVEA products. However, some 27 advertising agencies were responsible for developing the communication strategy for the individual product groups, and there was no coordination between these agencies. Despite similarities in several of the advertising campaigns, there was no consistent core statement or standardized design of the advertising.

As a result of permanently matching the communication of NIVEA *Creme* to current trends, the "Cartoon" campaign that had enjoyed 15 years of success (the goal of this campaign was to rejuvenate the NIVEA brand by means of association with early childhood memories, communicated with the help of naive paintings and the generation of pictures reminiscent of fairytales and supported by a special quality claim, such as "There's nothing better") was replaced in 1988 (on account of the results of a study) by the so-called "Lifestyle" campaign. This new campaign focused on the "individuality" of the consumers, and depicted people (e.g. attractive young women involved in sporting activities in a concentrated and self-aware fashion) who were thoroughly satisfied with their lives.

Despite the broad product range that has since emerged, NIVEA *Creme* continues to play a key role in the brand line. It is the mother of the NIVEA brand not only in terms of the biographical aspects, but also from a socio-historical standpoint (almost every consumer has already become acquainted with the brand during childhood, and consumers automatically associate the name NIVEA with NIVEA *Creme* – the blue tin). In 1992, roughly 22% of the overall turnover achieved with the NIVEA brand was attributable to NIVEA *Creme*.

This special role is also confirmed by two studies conducted at the start of the 1990s. The "Inner Visuals" imagery study conducted by the HTP Market Research Institute came to the conclusion that NIVEA – and NIVEA *Creme* in particular – possesses a high-level social image, which can most closely be described by terms such as family-oriented, tolerant and sincere. A second study concerning the socio-cultural values of consumers – performed by the RISC Group – reached the conclusion that values such as honesty, authenticity of sincere feelings and a return to family values are more important for the 1990s.

Questions

1. First of all, assess the baseline situation and subsequently elaborate the principles for a uniform brand policy and an international communication strategy.
2. Should Beiersdorf AG design an international communication strategy that is uniform for the entire brand line, or for one

product or product group only? What role should the brand
NIVEA *Creme* continue to play in this context? Propose a solution.
3. How should the communication strategy be designed? To this
   end, sketch a design concept for media advertising.

Acknowledgement

The authors would like to thank Mr Nortbert Krapp, Corporate Vice
President of Beiersdorf AG, for his kind support.

References and further reading

Aaker, D.A. (ed.) (1991) *Managing Brand Equity*. New York: Free Press.
Aaker, D.A. (ed.) (1996) *Building Strong Brands*. New York: Free Press.
Becker, J. (1994) Typen von Markenstrategien (types of brand strategies).
   In: Bruhn, M. (ed.) *Handbuch Markenartikel*, Vol. I, pp. 463–498.
   Stuttgart: Schäffer-Poeschel.
Berndt, R., Fantapié Altobelli, C. and Sander, M. (1995) Internationale
   Kommunikationspolitik (international communication policy). In:
   Hermanns, A. and Wißmeier, K. (eds) *Internationales Marketing-
   Management*, pp. 176–224. Munich: Vahlen.
Berndt, R., Fantapié Altobelli, C. and Sander, M. (1997) *Internationale
   Marketing-Politik* (international marketing policy). Berlin: Springer.
Hätty, H. (1994) Markentransferstrategie (Brand extension strategies). In:
   Bruhn, M. (ed.) *Handbuch Markenartikel*, Vol. I, pp. 561–582. Stuttgart:
   Schäffer-Poeschel.
HTP Research (ed.) (1990) *Nivea Creme-Bilder einer Marke*. München:
   Gesellschaft für Marktforschung.
Keller, K.L. (ed.) (1998) *Strategic Brand Management: Building, Measuring,
   and Managing Brand Equity*. Upper Saddle River, NJ: Prentice Hall.
Kotler, P. (ed.) (1997) *Marketing Management*, 9th edn. Englewood Cliffs,
   NJ: Prentice-Hall.
Meffert, H. and Bolz, J. (1998) *Internationales Marketing-Management*
   (international marketing management), 3rd edn. Stuttgart: Kohlhammer.
RISC (ed.) (1991) *The Guiding European Socio-Cultural Trends 1986–1990*.
   Nyon, Switzerland: International Research Institute on Social Change.

5

MCC: an innovative distribution strategy for an innovative product

Anina Busch and Joachim Mühlmeyer

Case	New product development
Main focus	Innovation
Subsidiary focus	Distribution, manufacturer–retailer partnership
Scene	European cities
Players	Car company, retailers, customers
Product	Electric car

Summary

The success of the innovative product "Smart" (a micro concept car) is not only based on innovative research and development in automotive techniques. New marketing and distribution strategies are absolutely essential in all industries. What can be learned from MCC's strategy and in particular its distribution systems?

Introduction

This case, which is still very much a going concern, gives a fascinating insight into the excitement, and difficulty, of both developing an innovative new product and introducing a new distribution system at the same time. It includes elements of shared funding and retail outlets, a new concept in car buying with instant, customized service, and a sophisticated after-sales service for an ecologically sound product.

It is autumn 1998 and Daimler Benz, after careful research into the demand for short-distance city cars carrying one or two people, are about to launch their product using retail outlets (and shared concepts) in conjunction with Swatch. From the customers' point of view, there is to be the opportunity to treat car purchase as "fun" – a low-priced product which can be bought almost on impulse and chosen with different coloured body parts and accessories. The cars are stored in transparent containers on a lift – open to view and easy to choose – and the "shops" will have multimedia displays and Swatch products to choose from while customers sip their coffee.

The idea is carefully spelled out from the design of outlets to the provision of back-up facilities and equipment for sales representations at point of sale. The theory is that with the Daimler Benz and Swatch combined experience of their markets, this combination of product and sales method cannot fail.

Warning notes are sounded: the sales partner has to make "unusually large investments" and carries the business risk. He also has "little scope for making his own decisions" but MCC is sure that in the long run its strategies – combining a needed product with a new distribution strategy – will prove attractive to its sales partners.

Readers will find this a useful way to look at the normal structure of the automobile industry and compare the ideas developed for Smart. Questions as to the "target customer" also repay discussion – should MCC and its partners be aiming at one "Euro customer" or will different markets have different target groups?

Will the distribution system and retail partner have to differ in the different countries?

KEYWORDS

Distribution strategy, sales organization, new game strategy, innovation, international marketing, solution marketing.

Case

Autumn 1998: The Smart, developed by MCC (Micro Compact Car), is introduced to the market. MCC is a joint venture between Daimler Benz and SMH/Swatch (Schweizerische Gesellschaft für Mikroelektronik und Uhrenindustrie AG). The Smart – the name is an amalgam of Swatch, Mercedes and Art – is not only an unusual and practical little car; it is the centre of an innovative, urban mobility concept.

The realization of such a project demands innovations which reach beyond scientific development and technical wizardry. In order to ensure the success of the Smart, a new marketing and distribution concept is needed.

BASIC IDEA OF THE SMART CONCEPT

The Smart concept stems from the enormous increase in inner city traffic. This is a worldwide phenomenon. Research shows that cars driven in inner city areas carry on average 1.2 passengers. Most second cars in a household only travel 10 000 miles (6250 kilometres) a year – less than 30 kilometres a day. This indicates that most cars in such areas travel short distances. If you include the time such a car is parked, stuck in a traffic jam or not in use, it is likely to stand still 90% of the time. MCC realized that the task of transportation of small numbers of people for short distances could be carried out by ecological cars that are much smaller than traditional cars. They have developed a totally new kind of vehicle that offers ecological advantages, relieves the pressure on inner city traffic, is easy on the household budget and fulfils the demands of urban mobility. At MCC the motto is: "We are not simply selling a car, but mobility". Smart is 2.5 metres long and has a 550-litre boot. Priced at between CHF12 000 and 16 000 (i.e. between about 7500 and 10 000 Euros) depending on the accessories, it is inexpensive, and has low fuel consumption (4.51 litres/100 kilometres). Despite its small size the Smart fulfils the demands for comfort and safety of most middle-sized cars. The idea of mobility includes other aspects of the marketing plan: immediate delivery at the point of sale, two-hour repair service, car-sharing, cooperation with car rental agencies, construction of special parking places for small vehicles and a "mobibox" in every vehicle, which provides access to communication and mobility services (e.g. navigation systems).

In order to make the Smart available at a competitive price, the highest degree of cost efficiency had to be attained at every level – from procurement to production and distribution, point of sale, and recycling. The demand for increased cost efficiency could only be satisfied by establishing a global marketing concept that enables the realization of these synergies.

The idea was that "price" should not be the main selling point. Being trendy was the aim: Smart is a lifestyle product. Bumpers, roof and hood are available in many different colours and can be combined individually by the customer. In addition, recurrent collections are planned. The car has thus been turned into a consumer good, that you own not only because you need it, but because it is trendy, rational and ecological. The aim is that the buyer shall be able to choose and take the car in the colour combination he or she prefers as soon as possible – preferably at once! In most cases orders for special colours and motor and accessory requirements have to be fulfilled spontaneously at the point of sale. To operate such an ordering and delivery service requires special logistic and service skills from the dealer.

This innovative and future-oriented concept was aimed at the customer target group of dynamic, modern and receptive people. Product appeal is to both rational and emotional elements that are valid across national borders. A Smart owner would wish to experience the same Smart-world in every country. The core target group includes singles and couples without children and with double income (DINKS). In addition, it is expected that the Smart will be attractive to families as a second or third car and to young-minded older people.

ESTIMATION OF THE MARKET FOR THE SMART

The Smart was positioned in the compact and sub-compact segment, defined by MCC as comprising cars shorter than 3.85 metres and costing less than CHF16 000. A boom phase is prognosticated for this segment up to 2000. After this, a start-up-analysis forecasted a sales volume of 200 000 Smarts per year from 2001 on. This sales target is equivalent to a market share of 6% of the small car segment. Because the vehicle is in fact intended to be urban (and only has two seats) this small car segment is perhaps not the most appropriate. "City car" might be a better description, and in that category, there are only three clear competitors to date: the Opel Max, the Ford Ka and the planned VW Lupo.

THE DISTRIBUTION STRATEGY

Demands such as immediate delivery, a global marketing concept and high logistic and service skills at point of service can hardly be realized within the traditional infrastructure of the car trade consisting as it does of small and relatively independent sales units and national importers. For this reason MCC has developed its own innovative distribution strategy. The main elements of this distribution strategy are the system of supporting points, the Smart-centres and the sales system.

THE SYSTEM OF SUPPORTING POINTS

The introduction of Smart on the market was set to take place in about 80 congested urban areas in the following European countries: Germany, France, Italy, Spain, Switzerland, Austria, Belgium, the Netherlands and Luxembourg. The 110 distribution areas would focus on large population areas and guarantee the dealers a big target audience. Steps were also taken to prevent dealers from competing with each other and neutralizing their marketing activities. Every distribution area was to be opened up with one sales partner using a modular system of supporting points (in comparison, the French autogroup Renault has 12 000 dealers in Europe). The system of supporting points consisted of regional Smart-centres, sales and service satellites. Table 5.1 shows the organization planned.

Communication satellites were originally planned as an additional module in the system of supporting points but it was decided not to implement them. Multimedia terminals were supposed to pass on information about the Smart and the supporting points at locations with high consumer frequencies such as airports and train stations. A field study showed that such communication satellites are scarcely

TABLE 5.1   Smart – the modular system of supporting points, 1998

	Description	Objective	Location
Smart-centre	Main point of sale for the product palette of the Smart Integrated service point	At least one Smart-centre in every distribution area is planned 4 sizes (max. area 4300 m², max. sales volume 1500 Smarts/year)	On the outskirts Close to high-traffic-areas, e.g. shopping malls Connection to the public transportation system
Sales satellite	Additional sales module for selected Smart models in order to cover the distribution area Selected offer of services	One or two sales satellites per distribution area according to the expected sales volume	In the city centre, at favourable locations with high customer frequency Connection to shopping malls
Service satellite	No sale Selected offer of services	Number of satellites decided by the sales partner with prior consultation of MCC	In the city centre In surrounding centres of population

Source: Management Zentrum, St Gallen, 1998.

used by the consumers. However, it was felt that for the time being a system of supporting points, consisting of the Smart-centre, the sales and the service satellites, should ensure intensive contact with customers.

THE SMART-CENTRE

The Smart is only available in the Smart-centre and the sales satellite. Just as the Smart does not want to be a conventional car, the Smart-centres also differ in many ways from traditional car sales points.

Architecture

The architecture of the Smart-centre reflects its corporate identity. The futuristic form of the Smart-centre is uniform Europe-wide and provides a distinct and unmistakable appearance for the "Smart" brand. The smooth and fast Europe-wide implementation of the Smart-architecture concept is enabled by a large number of prefabricated steel elements. Apart from this futuristic architectural concept, the centres use resource-saving building material and economic use of energy. The core element of the Smart-centre is the "car-tower", a huge glass rack, in which up to 45 cars can be stored and exhibited at the same time. A computer-controlled lift stores cars which can be supplied within minutes (or kept until needed). Other rooms for sales, repair, administration and trade of used cars are grouped around the car-tower.

The presentation ambience

It is hoped that the customer's choice of vehicle should be made easier with a positive and enjoyable shopping experience. Sales personnel are to follow the guideline "giving advice instead of selling". MCC has developed special communication instructions for the point of sale that support the consultative service of the sales personnel and offer the customer innovative and playful opportunities for information and product identification.

One fundamental element of this communication concept at the point of sale is the use of interactive media. In order to create the shopping experience, the Smart-centres were to have a bistro/café area, open to both customers and passers-by. The integration of a Swatch sales point in every Smart-centre was also planned. Swatch watches fit into the Smart philosophy and are supposed to be an interesting extra offer for the customer. In the accessories shop the full range of accessories for the vehicle will be exhibited.

Customer orientation was not to end with the act of purchase; the goal is to enter a long-term cooperative relationship with the customer by using special service offers, customer events and updating packages and accessories to the car.

THE SMART DISTRIBUTION SYSTEM

Thus, with Smart, Europe was to see a distribution network for automobiles that did not use the traditional infrastructure of the car industry with its independent dealers. A modern business strategy demands the implementation of a modern distribution system. In cooperation between MCC and its sales partners there was no intermediary or additional wholesaler level. The Smart was not introduced to different markets by national import companies; instead the Smart sales partner was to order vehicles, accessories and spare parts directly from the Smart production plant and handle the market in direct cooperation with MCC. The Smart plant is located in Hambach in Lorraine, France.

The selection of sales partners

Demands on Smart sales partners were to be high. A Smart sales partner would need to be an entrepreneur with an extensive range of attributes: a car dealer and an importer with marketing, communication and logistic skills. Financial power would also be relevant. The partner should be able to raise an equity of at least CHF2 million. Another important criterion for the selection of a sales partner would be personality: MCC looked for partners with leadership qualities. They had to prove their entrepreneurial leadership skills and have experience of dealing cars or other branded products. The requirements were consciously set at a high level, to avoid applicants who were looking only for a short-term profit and not interested in engaging in the long-term establishment of a successful brand. In spite of the high personal, entrepreneurial and financial requirements, partners were found for 95% of the distribution areas.

Obligations of MCC and the sales partners

As in any partnership the Smart distribution system was founded on mutual obligations. The MCC ensured the sales partner the exclusive right to distribute the product and service combinations in a defined distribution area. The activities of the partner were concentrated accordingly on the product and service palette of MCC, including the sale of new vehicles, the provision of spare parts, the repair of vehicles and the sale of service packages.

MCC was to be responsible for the implementation of an integrated quality management that complied with the requirements of ISO

9001. (For a definition of the International Standardization Organization numbers, see Stauss (1994).) Furthermore, MCC was to make its know-how available to the sales partner through a catalogue containing entrepreneurial consulting services and specially coordinated management tools. This was to include hardware and software packages, training programmes, support in recruiting and promoting personnel, for example. In addition, knowledge transfer was also to be supported by an active company-wide exchange of experiences initiated by MCC.

MCC also established a uniform customer and vehicle database in order to reduce the cost of acquiring essential information for the sales partner. The communication concept is developed centrally, but gives the sales partners room for regional adjustments. Support for customer communication, advertising, promotion and the layout of the point of sale and specific merchandising offers were supplied to the sales partner at low cost.

MCC helped its partners to select the right location and supported the construction of the sales point. Following strategic aspects, appropriate locations for the modular system of supporting points were evaluated and conveyed. MCC delivered construction plans and supervised the entire construction process. Solutions for the interior design were also offered to the sales partner. Through these supporting services a rapid entry into the market was to be promoted. Sales partners commited themselves to pay a sign-up-fee and a fixed proportion of the annual gross turnover to MCC.

New definition of the relationship of manufacturer and sales partner

The new distribution set up for Smart aimed to define a new relationship between manufacturer and sales partner which would be bound to become close. To guarantee the company-wide exchange of experience in market research, product strategies, advertising campaigns etc., an advisory board with selected sales partners would be formed. The exchange of experiences in this committee would guarantee optimal customer orientation and quality assurance.

The direct manufacturer/sales partner relationship ensures that the sales partner gets a fair share of the profit. It is only in the context of such a direct contact that low prices and additional benefits can be guaranteed to the customer. Corresponding with this increased responsibility, the sales partners' active right to influence the business policy would also increase. Short and direct communication routes would allow an immediate influence on the strategic orientation of the company, the sales support and marketing activities, which are tasks of MCC. The sales partners were assisted by a regional manager. They supported the sales partners in complying with business plans and implementing national and regional communication concepts. The regional manager provides experience and information with regard to operative activities and is the most important link to MCC. The uniform image of the product and the company is internationally secured by contract.

CONCLUDING THOUGHTS ABOUT SMART

The "Smart" concept represents an extensive combination of products and services, which allow transport solutions suited to the individual city car traveller. The combination of different design elements defines both product and corporate identity. The distribution strategy, with the strict licensing of MCC's products and the marketing concepts, aims to guarantee the quality and integrity of all the elements which contribute to the "Smart" concept, the company, its sales partners and the customers.

The MCC

- Avoids potential conflict with independent dealers and secures a uniform market appearance
- Achieves a high market penetration without having to invest vast financial resources in the dealerships

The sales partner

- Can rely on the technical and entrepreneurial know-how of MCC
- Has a well-founded basis for good performance in the market
- Has to undertake unusually large investments and at the same time carries the whole business risk
- Has little scope for making his or her own decisions

In short, the influence of MCC is far-reaching and decisive and the intensive cooperation between MCC and its sales partners enables an exploitation of synergies and an efficient cultivation of the market.

MCC is convinced that its distribution strategy in the long run will meet the expectations of the sales partners. Current trends in the car industry such as the low rates of return to the conventional automobile distribution network, the general lack of relationship management between the manufacturer and dealers and insufficient coordination of different market trends strongly influenced the distribution decisions. The new network was established for Smart through the system of supporting points.

WHAT HAPPENED NEXT?

An article in *CASH* (1999) tells us what happened next. The first Smarts were sold in October 1998. Break-even target was 160 000 sales. However, the Swatch group (SMH) pulled out of the joint venture with MCC shortly after the launch and technical problems with the product required an estimated minimum of CHF250 million in improvements. Sales did not reach expected levels. Between October and December 1998 only 19 000 Smarts were sold and the initial targeted special markets (Paris, Rome, Barcelona) had nowhere near the level of sales hoped for.

MCC introduced a variety of measures in response. Planned production for 1999 was reduced by 20% (from 130 000 to 100 000). New models – convertible and diesel and even a rumoured four-seater – are also being developed.

Questions

1. Describe the traditional distribution forms in the automobile industry and compare them to the distribution strategy of the Smart. Point out the innovative aspects.
2. What are the critical factors of success for the realization of the Smart concept?
3. In international marketing a decision has to be made to follow either a local strategy or a global standardized strategy. Develop

solutions as to how MCC can ensure customer orientation internationally and can profit as well from the advantages of marketing standardization.

4. The idea of the Smart is based on the construction of a Smart-world, characterized by mobility, lifestyle and innovation. Find innovative ideas how MCC could optimize the Smart-world in the future.

5. In the short run, what do you see to be the main problem confronting the sales development of Smart?

References and further reading

Ahlert, D. (1996) *Distributionspolitik*. Stuttgart: Schaeffer Poeschel.

Backhaus, K. (1996) *Internationales Marketing*. Stuttgart: Schaeffel Poeschel.

Belz, C., Muller, F. and Muller, R. (1996) Euromarketing – ein Zwischenfazit. In: *Thexis – Fachzeitschrift für Marketing*, No. 1, Se. 2–8. St Galen: Thexis.

Belz, C. (1998) *Akzente im innovativen Marketing*. St Gallen: Thexis.

Busch, R., Dogl, R. and Unger, F. (1995) *Integriertes Marketing*. Wiesbaden: Gabler.

CASH (1999) Issue 10, March 12.

Gilbert, X. and Strebel, P.J. (1987) Strategies to outpace competition. *Journal of Business Strategy*, No. 1.

Hamel, G. and Prahalad, C.K. (1995) *Wettlauf um die Zukunft*. Vienna: Ueberreuter.

Keagan, W.J. and Green, M.C. (1997) *Principles of Global Marketing*. New York: Prentice Hall.

Kotler, P. and Bliemel, F. (1999) *Marketing-Management*. Stuttgart: Schaeffer Poeschel.

Stauss, B. (1994) Qualitätsmanagement und Zertifizierung von DIN ISO 9000 zum Total Quality Management. Wiesbaden: Gabler.

Weinhold, H., Reinecke, S. and Schogel M. (eds) (1997) *Marketingdynamik*. St Gallen: Thexis.

6

The mixed blessings of the Euro

Yvonne van Everdingen and Ad Pruyn

Case	Effect of financial systems on marketing
Main focus	Company organization
Subsidiary focus	Advertising, commmunications, pricing
Scene	The Netherlands, EU entrants to EMU
Players	Government, small companies, retailers, consumer
Product	Currency

Summary

This case discusses the problems retailers will be faced with before, during and after the introduction of one single European currency: the Euro. Apart from administrative, legal and personnel consequences, for retail management there will be quite a number of costs involved in the introduction of the Euro. Specific marketing problems concern (psychological) pricing decisions related to the conversion of national currency to Euros, communication with customers during the transitional period, and problems of dual pricing (such as the adaptation of cash registers, scales and trolleys). As regards the provision of information to the public, the role of national governments is discussed.

© 2000 John Wiley & Sons, Ltd.
Understanding Marketing: A European Casebook edited by Celia Phillips, Ad Pruyn and Marie-Paule Kestemont.

Introduction

Here is a genuine euro-marketing case: how will the introduction of the Euro to 11 of the EU members affect both the business world and the general public?

Two main aspects are considered:

- The question of the organization of companies to respond to this change (and in particular the six-month period when the countries involved will have two legal tenders – their own national currency and the new Euro)
- The problem of communication of a change which will be implemented fairly soon

The authors begin by pointing out that while large international companies may welcome the Euro and the easy accounting and distribution systems it will bring, for the consumer and the small retailer, matters may be more muddled in the short term. They point out that most public information provided from 1996 has focused on those companies which would be the main beneficiaries rather than the other groups who need reassurance.

Figures from a 1998 survey show that attitudes towards the Euro among the general public in EU countries were variable, but actual awareness was low in most of them. The problems which will confront the retailer are then clearly spelled out.

The interest in this case lies in a very specific problem – how will customers and companies respond to changes in the marketing process in their countries? This is not the short-term problem it may sound. Over a period of years, countries which did not participate in the January 1999–July 2002 change will watch the dynamics of this development and make their own decisions to apply to join. Even after the process is complete, the implications of a larger common currency area will continue to need to be explored.

Questions set cover organizational issues and communication strategies and form the basis for a challenging European marketing class.

KEYWORDS

Euro, retailing, small- and medium-sized companies, psychological and international pricing, communication campaigns.

Case

INTRODUCTION

While large exporting firms are more than happy with the idea of the EMU, smaller companies feel they may be getting a raw deal. "We'll have to wait and see whether we will recover our costs at all."

In the Netherlands there was little debate about the EMU, partly because its opponents were fragmented. The main reason for the absence of any real discussion, however, is that almost everyone agrees that the EMU is good for the Netherlands. Eventually, both trade and industry and the general public would profit from a common currency and monetary union. But is this really true? Does this really apply to all of us? And if it doesn't, who will profit and who will not?

Rients Abma, secretary of economic affairs at the Dutch Employers Federation (VNO-NCW), has described the studies by The Bank of the Netherlands (De Nederlandse Bank) showing that the main winners will be those industries which relate to exporting and the international sector which will face lower risks and exchange rate costs and treasury administration costs. Retailers, on the other hand, will see fewer advantages but will be faced with higher costs, particularly during the transitional phase. In the first six months of 2002, both the Dutch guilder and the Euro will circulate with all the consequent drawbacks for retailers (double cash registers, sales slips in different currencies, two separate bookkeepings, etc.). (VNO/NCW 1996.)

Wout Vogelesang (EIM Research) agrees with Abma. "Based on a study we carried out in conjunction with KPMG, we estimate that for Dutch retailers the costs will amount to three billion Dutch florins (DFL): two billion guilders will be spent on administrative preparations, cash registers, slot machines and so on, and one billion will be needed during the transition itself. . . Additional employees will be needed, as well as new equipment, and software will have to be adapted." Vogelesang also points to prices. "Eventually", he says, "the retailer will have to completely reconsider his pricing strategy." With a precise conversion of guilders to Euros, one may end up with strange figures (different to the well known such as DFL1.79). And it will of course be impossible to employ different prices for one and the same product in the transitional period when customers can pay in guilders or Euros. Nor will it be accepted that all prices are adjusted in an upward direction after the transitional period, during which Vogelesang expects "consumer unions to be pouncing on price tags".

(Lof 1998. Translated by the authors and reproduced with permission.)

TIME PATH FOR THE REPLACEMENT OF NATIONAL CURRENCIES BY
THE EURO

The Economic and Monetary Union (EMU) was founded to establish
cooperation and integration of economic and monetary politics
between the member states of the European Union. Its ultimate goal
was the introduction of a common European currency, the Euro.
During a meeting in May 1998, the financial ministers from several
European governments agreed that the EMU would start with 11
countries from 1 January 1999. Countries not joining the EMU from
the beginning are Greece (which did not meet the convergence
criteria set by the Maastricht Treaty), and the United Kingdom,
Denmark and Sweden (which, for the time being, have decided to
stay out of the EMU, voluntarily).

So 1 January 1999 saw the introduction of the Euro as an accounting unit (eurocoins and notes did not yet exist as legal tender).
However, from this date, all bank transfers were to take place in Euro
currency. In addition, companies from non-EMU countries can
choose to open Euro-accounts in order to be able to deal in Euros
with their trading partners, although they are not obliged to do so.

Eurocoins – and notes – will be introduced in all participating
countries three years after the introduction, on 1 of January 2002.
National currencies are to be completely replaced by the Euro, on 1
July 2002, at the latest. This means that during the first six months of
the year 2002, eurocoins and notes will be used side-by-side with
existing European currencies, which will lead to many practical
problems, for both consumers and retailers. After 1 July, national
currencies in the participating countries will no longer be legal
tender.

INFORMATION CAMPAIGNS BY NATIONAL GOVERNMENTS

Despite the far-reaching consequences of these developments, it
appeared that both companies and the general public were badly
informed about the possible consequences of EMU even a few years
before the beginning of EMU. Results of a number of studies conducted among Dutch companies at the end of 1996 revealed that not
only did small companies feel uninformed about the consequences

of the Euro (about 70% said they were), but also about 50% of large companies indicated that they were relatively uninformed (e.g. VNO/NCW 1996; Euroteam 1996). In so far as they had information on the Euro their most important sources of information appeared not to be the national government, but private banks and professional journals. Moreover, several representatives of small- and medium-sized enterprises called for public authorities to develop specific programmes to assist them with technical aspects of the changeover and to provide specific information programmes targeting their needs.

In addition, an international study investigating the attitudes of European citizens/consumers towards the Euro revealed a lack of knowledge (Müller-Peters et al. 1998). Most people interviewed seemed to have no idea about the value of the Euro, while many respondents expected the introduction of the actual Euro to be well *before* the year 2002. Although people from all European countries displayed low levels of knowledge, the Italians, Portuguese, Greeks, Irish, British, Danish and Swedish appeared to be particularly uninformed.

This is particularly worrying in the case of those countries that are joining the system from the start. Dutch and German citizens, on the other hand, showed above average knowledge about the Euro.

In addition, there are interesting cross-national differences in attitudes toward the Euro. People from countries such as Spain, Italy, Ireland and Belgium appeared to be in favour of the Euro, while the British, Swedish, Danish and Germans showed much more scepticism about its introduction.

The European Commission and national governments started their information campaigns during 1996. They aimed first at the banking industry and multinational companies, and neglected retailers and public education. Only in 1998, after it was decided which countries would participate in EMU from 1999, were campaigns developed in each of these countries to inform the broader public about the Euro. However, the results of the studies previously discussed had already indicated that at the start of the EMU a great deal still had to be done, both to inform the public about the process of moving to the single currency, and to help companies in preparing for this changeover to a single currency.

RETAILERS AND THE EURO

As may be clear from the quotation at the beginning of this case, retailers will encounter many problems when they have to introduce the Euro, while they cannot expect as many advantages as international companies. This case will therefore focus on the expected consequences and the necessary preparatory actions for retailers in particular.

They can expect four broad categories of consequences.

- *First, retailers will have to deal with a number of administrative problems.* Here, one may think of the translation of all relevant price information to Euros in the company's administration: bookkeeping systems, price lists, invoices, etc. Hard- and software, such as cash registers, scales, and penny-in-the-slot machines, will also have to be adjusted to the new currency.
- *Secondly, retailers will be confronted with a number of legal consequences.* These particularly relate to existing contracts. Contracts in EU currencies that will disappear will not cause a great problem, since these can be easily translated to the Euro. However, contracts with partners not joining EMU might cause problems, if these partners are reluctant to accept a changeover to the Euro. Another legal consequence concerns the rounding off procedures involved in the conversion of national currencies to Euros. As decreed by the European Union Council, the Euro exchange rate should be expressed in six decimals (no rounding off!), and after conversion new Euro prices (in three decimals) should be rounded off to the nearest Eurocent. Rounding off procedures may affect profits considerably, especially in food retail where margins on products are often small.
- *A third category of consequences relates to personnel.* It is expected that additional personnel will be necessary for a while. With customers able to pay with a mixture of national currency and Euros, longer queues at cashiers' checkouts are likely. Training of shop staff will need considerable attention. Front-line retail personnel can be expected to be called to account by customers when they suspect irregularities in price conversions, or when (double) price information needs further explanation.

All the necessary changes related to administration, legal affairs and personnel will entail high costs, which are estimated as ranging from 1.1% to 4.2% of retailers' total turnover (Vogelesang and Stroes 1997).

- *A fourth category of consequences relates to marketing, in-store communication and sales.* Bottlenecks may involve pricing decisions (double pricing: how long and how; psychological pricing and problems of rounding off; compatibility and transparency of international pricing), dealing with different currencies (the design of tills, sales slips, price tags, etc.) and the adaptation of existing customer logistics (such as deposits, coupons and loyalty programmes, free-gift systems, etc.). Also, choices have to be made with respect to the most appropriate moments of preparation.

Questions

CONSEQUENCES OF THE EURO FOR RETAILERS

1. In general, how do you think consumers will react to the introduction of the Euro? To what extent and how will this introduction affect consumers' price perceptions? Is there any reason to anticipate international differences in consumer reactions to the Euro?
2. Describe the problems a retailer will encounter in the different stages (three periods: before, during and after the transition) of the changeover to the Euro. What kind of solutions do you propose?
3. Design a communication strategy for your customers. How could you assist your customers both before and during the transition period? Do you think there are reasons for segmentation of customer groups as concerns the help they need? Why?
4. What (dis)advantages can be associated to either a long (e.g. six months) or a short ("big bang") transition period? As a retailer, what would you prefer? And as a consumer?

INFORMATION PROVIDED BY GOVERNMENTAL INSTITUTIONS

1. Why do you think the information campaign of national govern-
    ments was focused initially on large multinationals and banks,
    and only at a later stage on retailers and citizens? Do you think
    governments were right to do this?
2. What kind of information do retailers need? Make a distinction
    between the period before the introduction of the chartal Euro
    (coins and notes), the period in which dual currencies exist, and
    the period after the national currency is completely replaced by
    the Euro.
3. Should all countries use the same standardized campaign, or
    should the information campaigns be adapted to local circum-
    stances?

References and further reading

Euroteam (1996) *Invoering van de Euro*. Internal report, Moret Ernst &
    Young, Euroteam/Erasmus University.
Lof, E. (1998) Het verdeelde genoegen van de Euro (The mixed blessings of
    the Euro). *Intermediair* 30 April.
Müller-Peters, A., Pepermans, R., Kiell, G. et al. (1998) Explaining attitudes
    towards the Euro: Design of a cross-national study. *Journal of Economic
    Psychology* 19: 663–680.
VNO/NCW (1996) *Onderzoek Euro*. Internal report of the VNO.
Vogelesang, W.J.P. and Stroes, B.J.F. (1997) *Modellering effecten invoering
    Euro. Fase 1: analyse van de kosten*. Den Haag: Hoofbedrijfsschap
    Detailhandel.

7

Integrating brand strategies after an acquisition: Schwarzkopf & Henkel cosmetics

Axel Faix, Anne Christin Kemper and Richard Köhler

Case	Brand repositioning
Main focus	Marketing mix, target group (or market segmentation, customer segmentation)
Subsidiary focus	International marketing, pricing, advertising
Scene	Germany, worldwide
Players	Company, brands, consumers
Product	Cosmetics – shampoo

Summary

For many years, Gliss Kur and Poly Kur were competing brands which represented Schwarzkopf GmbH and Henkel KgaA, their respective companies, in the hair-care market. Now that Henkel has acquired Schwarzkopf, how should Schwarzkopf & Henkel Cosmetics treat these former competitors? What strategies should be adopted to achieve maximum exploitation of market potentialities? How can the new brand concept rooted in both companies be implemented at an international level? What positioning strategy should be adopted in order to avoid duplicating brand positions?

© 2000 John Wiley & Sons, Ltd.
Understanding Marketing: A European Casebook edited by Celia Phillips,
Ad Pruyn and Marie-Paule Kestemont.

Introduction

Here is another case set in the cosmetics industry and specifically in the market for hair shampoo and a brand repositioning problem. Readers are introduced to two brands which having for many years been rivals (and indeed, although from different original "stables", have similar names) are now products of the same company. The challenge to their owner Schwarzkopf & Henkel is how to target them in such a way that they complement each other and increase profits for the company rather than competing in a wasteful manner.

The relationship between price and the degree of specialization of various competitor and ideal products is shown and we are introduced to three ideal brands and their main target groups. Ideas of communicating the two brands and possible pricing strategies given possible different segments for targeting are examined. In the end, however, Gliss and Poly Kur failed to develop a separate identity in the period immediately after the Henkel acquisition of Schwarzkopf. How should they develop a new brand policy? In a rapidly changing world, this is a problem which arises again and again as new mergers and acquisitions take place at a national and international level.

Readers may find it helpful to supplement the questions set on brand repositioning in this case by considering one or two imminent or recent such changes in their own marketing environment and considering the implications these will have and the research they might need to initiate in order to evaluate such developments.

KEYWORDS

Acquisition, brand, brand strategy, differentiation, elimination, international marketing, marketing mix, positioning, product policy, target group.

Case

In 1997, Henkel owned a total of 330 companies and had nearly 55 000 employees in over 60 countries. It generated sales of DM20.1 billion (about 10.28 billion Euros) through its six product market sectors *Adhesives, Detergents/Household Cleansers, Cosmetics/ Toiletries, Surface Technologies, Chemical Products* and *Industrial and Institutional Hygiene.*

The *Cosmetics/Toiletries* sector generated sales of DM2.97 billion in 1997. Here activities are dominated by the need to integrate a former competitor (Hans Schwarzkopf GmbH). The shares of Schwarzkopf (a descendant of the company founder) initially derived from Hoechst AG (1995) and Schwarzkopf was then bought out by Henkel in 1996. In its last year as a separate company, Hans Schwarzkopf GmbH achieved world sales of over one billion Deutschmarks and had a workforce of more than 4000 employees.

Following the acquisition of Schwarzkopf by Henkel the *branded articles business* in the Cosmetics/Toiletries sector, which includes the strategic business units Body Care, Oral Hygiene, Skin Care and Fragrances, has been regrouped as *Schwarzkopf & Henkel Cosmetics* (SHC). The hair salon business, however, is represented by *Schwarzkopf Professional.* SHC's international alignment is reflected in over 50 affiliated companies in 44 countries.

Following the acquisition, SHC faced problems in the hair-care sector. They needed to reorganize the marketing of three main brands, one, *Poly Kur*, which originated with Henkel and two, *Gliss Kur* and *Schauma*, which had been part of the Schwarzkopf portfolio. They needed to avoid mutual interference on the market and to achieve the best possible exploitation of market potential. The relevant decisions relating to mid 1997 (i.e. the period roughly six months after finalization of the acquisition) focus on designing their future brand strategy, including implementation in terms of marketing policy and international marketing considerations. Brand policy considerations centre around the necessity to analyse respective *brand positioning* of the three products and to draft design recommendations on the basis of these analyses.

The *positioning* of a brand is the position it occupies in the eyes of consumers in comparison with ideal and competing brands.

- Analysing the *actual position* involves identifying the position of real and ideal brands in terms of criteria governing the decision to buy, as subjectively perceived by consumers in a multi-dimensional awareness and evaluation context.

- This is followed by the specification of the *target positioning*, the most essential aspect of which is the position assessed by the consumers as ideal (*ideal brand*).
- Depending on the position of a company's brand in relation to the ideal brand, efforts can then be focused on *reinforcing* or *shifting the actual brand position* nearer to the ideal brand.
- In principle, it would also be conceivable to *influence the ideal requirements* to bring them into line with the company's brand.

So far as competitors are concerned this decision-making problem can be expressed as the choice between a *profiling strategy* (to distinguish oneself from the competition by a unique selling proposition and to occupy a positioning niche) and an *imitative* or *"me too"* strategy.

The decision to buy in the hair-care sector is primarily determined by three dimensions.

- The first is the *brand price positioning (pricing)*.
- The second is the *performance basis*. This can stress the "natural quality" i.e. when hair problems are solved by products providing more gentle, mild care through vegetable ingredients. Another option would be to offer "high-tech" products which provide a pronounced "technical" repair performance on the basis of scientific know-how.
- The third evaluation dimension is the *perceived degree of specialization* of the brand, as reflected in the differentiation of the products offered. This is determined on the one hand by the breadth of the product range, i.e. the number and types of product variants for different *hair types* and *problems* (e.g. fine, dry/stressed, permed/dyed hair), and on the other hand by the depth of the range, represented by the care performance intensity or the number and types of *application varieties* for hair problems (instant repair treatment, pack, thermal pack, revitalizing care, etc.). Brands occupying a specialist position are those which not only provide products for a great many hair types and problems, but also offer a large number of differentiated application varieties for problem hair (with graduated action

intensity). The general brands focus on normal hair-care (e.g. family products), with a small number of product variants and application varieties.

Figure 7.1 illustrates the positioning of Gliss Kur, Poly Kur and Schauma in 1997 in comparison with competing and ideal brands in terms of the feature dimensions explained above. The positions assessed as ideal are based on SHC Management estimates. Note that their market research shows that performance basis is less significant in terms of decision to buy than the other two dimensions. This is shown by the different degrees of shading in the figure.

The figure shows a clear relationship between source and perceived quality. Consumers are basically prepared to pay high prices for what they perceive as special care performance. The various positions of the three *ideal brands* relate to different *market segments* as possible target groups.

- In the zone around ideal brand I, the predominant group comprises hair-care consumers looking for a reasonably priced general brand for themselves or their families.
- The ideal brand II segment relates to persons (especially women) aged between 20 and 40 in the middle income bracket who prefer uncomplicated but effective hair-care.
- Ideal brand III mainly relates to women in the higher income bracket who expect more in terms of hair-care performance. The age of these women also ranges widely (between 20 and 55).

Ideal brand III is of particular interest because demographic studies in most European countries show that the proportion of the population over 40 years of age will increase sharply in the future. SHC market research studies also indicate that this age group has high purchasing power and that it will probably develop increased awareness of appearance and health in the coming years. Promising products in this segment will have to cater to the special problems of older people, e.g. less resilient or thinning hair, and hair loss. It is apparent that increasing numbers of people are now ready to use a more technological type of product in the hair-care segment.

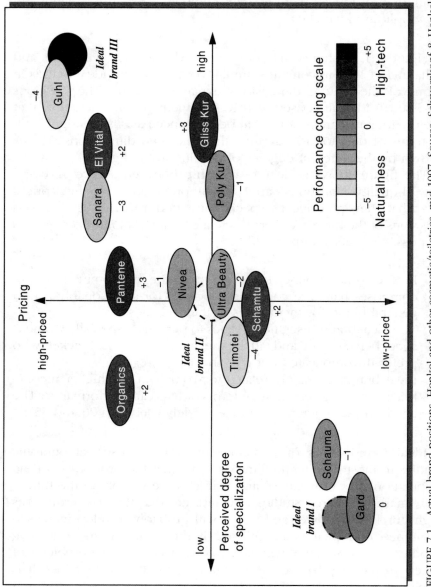

FIGURE 7.1 Actual brand positions, Henkel and other cosmetic/toiletries, mid-1997. Source: Schwarzkopf & Henkel, in-house. Reproduced by their permission.

So far as SHC brands are concerned, Figure 7.1 also shows that, following the acquisition, Henkel now has two brands with similar positioning, Gliss Kur and Poly Kur. Schauma is quite differently positioned. As a result, this case will concentrate mainly on problems relating to the Gliss Kur and Poly Kur brands.

As far as the *performance basis* is concerned, Gliss Kur (the original Schwarzkopf brand) and Poly Kur (the original Henkel brand) occupy different positions, since Gliss Kur focuses more on the *high-tech* aspects of the product, whereas Poly Kur is characterized by its *natural quality*. However, it should be remembered that due to several relaunches and repositioning campaigns in the years prior to Henkel's acquisition of Schwarzkopf – some of which tended towards increased high-tech competence – Poly Kur lines are not clearly perceived as being natural care products. Poly Kur still conjures up technical associations. Gliss Kur, on the other hand, is a highly specialized brand which has consistently been engineered as a high-tech product promising consumers high competence based on outstanding, scientifically substantiated hair repair performance.

In terms of *pricing*, both brands are situated in the medium price range, though consumers do not rate Poly Kur's price/performance ratio as excellent as that of Gliss Kur. SHC experts estimate that consumers associate Gliss Kur with a high level of treatment competence and will therefore be more willing to accept higher prices without switching to other brands. This willingness is not as pronounced in the case of Poly Kur.

The very similar *degree of specialization* is due to the similarity of the assortment structure of Gliss Kur and Poly Kur in the segments of shampoos, care products (conditioners), conventional hair treatments (e.g. packs), and special treatments (e.g. hair-end fluids). The vast breadth and above all the depth of the assortments confers on both brands the *position of a hair-care specialist* in the treatment segment. Poly Kur has a slightly wider range for many of the relatively normal hair types but a slightly narrower range of special treatments. Gliss Kur's assortment includes highly differentiated products for hair types and focuses on special applications for different, but mostly problem hair. The unique selling proposition of the Gliss Kur brand stems from this differentiation. Poly Kur, on the other hand, is mainly oriented toward uncomplicated care for a wide variety of hair types.

In summary, as a result of consistent brand management, Gliss Kur is reckoned to have significantly higher competence in the repair and special treatments segment for different types of problem hair. For some time now, SHC has been considering introducing special products to meet the specific care needs of older people. Figure 7.2 illustrates the Gliss Kur and Poly Kur assortment structures graphically after the Schwarzkopf acquisition. As the figure shows, they overlap to a considerable extent.

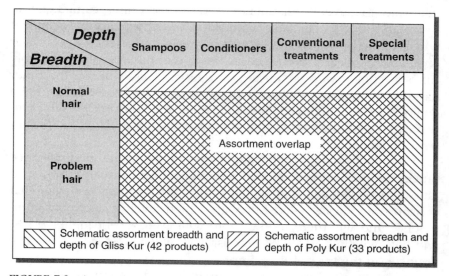

FIGURE 7.2   Assortment structure of Gliss Kur and Poly Kur after the Henkel/ Schwarzkopf acquisition (1997). Source: Schwarzkopf & Henkel, in-house. Reproduced by their permission.

If one looks at the *marketing mix design*, it can be seen that *product policy specifications* for Poly Kur include the use of formulations incorporating vegetable ingredients, but without any consistent reflection of this in the *packaging design*.

Over a long period, the bottles used for conditioners and shampoos, for example, tended to have a rectangular outline. Only relatively recently has an attempt been made to give the bottles a more "natural" character by adding the picture of a leaf. In contrast,

Gliss Kur products include substances claimed to provide chemical repair performance, which has been stressed since 1996 by the keywords "Hair Repair Complex". Packaging for Gliss Kur products consistently features a pictorial motif of stylized hair repair.

The idea of introducing products catering to the hair problems of the 40-plus age group is currently being deliberated. Within the scope of a new concept called the "Age Repair 40+" line, formulations are being developed which will include *vita proteins* (vitamin–protein complexes) as ingredients. Initial market research results indicate a high level of acceptance for this care line.

When *communicating* for Poly Kur products, the focus since the last repositioning has concentrated on *natural* care properties. The Gliss Kur brand is now increasingly targeting demanding consumers with a high interest in cosmetics (this being partly due to the great similarity with the Poly Kur target group). The intention is to draw these consumers' attention to the fact that, with problem hair, the "Hair Repair Complex" is the only alternative to cutting the hair. This is underlined in communication by a visual message, with scissors symbolizing the drastic last resort.

As already described, product *pricing* is basically similar for both brands, with Gliss Kur commanding slightly higher prices. The explanation given by SHC experts for the particularly pronounced price acceptance for a special care line for older people is the higher purchasing power of this target group and their tendency to pay more for special performance. The *distribution policy* for Gliss Kur and Poly Kur focuses on wide distribution of the products in both cases, with special emphasis on chemists and specialized retailers.

At the *international* level, Gliss Kur and Poly Kur products are mainly sold in Western Europe with inroads now also being made in Eastern European countries. The findings presented here come from in-house work by SHC on its products (1998). Apart from a few countries such as Russia and Poland, where special circumstances prevail due to the economic development in these countries, the target countries are generally similar in terms of economic factors (e.g. gross domestic product, purchasing power, competition and media situation), legal and political considerations (e.g. laws, regulations), geographical conditions (e.g. climate, topography), technological fundamentals of production, as well as socio-cultural factors (e.g. consumer habits and attitudes to cosmetic articles). For example, the attitude to using hair-care products is usually rather uncomplicated as regards the potential benefits obtained through using these products (healthy hair, personal attractiveness, etc.). In this context, however, SHC market research results indicate that the picture of a sophisticated, experienced consumer of hair-care products is more typical of German-speaking than French-speaking countries.

In the period after the acquisition, SHC noted that Gliss Kur and Poly Kur were not developing as desired on the market and that there was interdependence in both entrepreneurial planning and market-oriented implementation. Product management is therefore faced with the problem of designing virtually the same concepts for two similarly positioned, but practically competing brands. The sales department cannot find sufficient arguments to push distribution of both brands in the trade. This is particularly the case in the special treatments segment where the products are essentially similar.

Gliss Kur and Poly Kur also compete in terms of consumer preference, since the specialist positioning plays a greater role in the decision to buy than questions of natural quality or scientific care performance. Considerable substitution to the debit of Poly Kur is therefore probable, and this is worsened by the similarity of the Gliss Kur and Poly Kur target groups. SHC has decided, however, to maintain both brands. Its problem is therefore how to develop a new brand policy for them.

Questions

1. Devise a suitable new (target) positioning for the two brands, referring to the three positioning dimensions mentioned above.
2. Explain the consequences of the new positioning for the assortment structures of Gliss Kur and Poly Kur, making suggestions for an appropriate breadth and depth of the brands' assortment (with regard to their intended degree of specialization).
3. What conclusions can be drawn from the proposed positioning for the implementation in terms of marketing measures?

Acknowledgements

The authors would like to thank Dr Rainer W. Schmidt and Andrea Schwalbach at Henkel KGaA for their kind support.

References and further reading

Cravens, D.W. (1997) *Strategic Marketing*, 5th edn. Chicago, IL: Irwin.

Köhler, R. (1993) *Beiträge zum Marketing-Management (Contributions to Marketing Management)*, 3rd edn. Stuttgart: Schäffer-Poeschel.

Lambin, J.-J. (1997) *Strategic Marketing Management*, 2nd edn. London: McGraw-Hill.

Ries, A. and Trout, J. (1986) *Positioning. The Battle for Your Mind*. London: McGraw-Hill.

Wall Street Journal (1995) Henkel to buy hair-care unit from Hoechst, August 12.

Waltermann, B. (1989) *Internationale Markenpolitik und Produktpositionierung (International Brand Management and Product Positioning)*. Vienna: Service.

8

Perrier: the benzene crisis

Josep Franch and Jordi Montaña

Case	Crisis management
Main focus	Global brand, communications
Subsidiary focus	Ethics, corporate image
Scene	USA
Players	Company president, health regulations, consumers
Product	Mineral water

Summary

The President of Perrier is unlikely to forget Friday, 9 February 1990. Traces of benzene had been found in bottles of Perrier – and the news spread like wildfire. Perrier customers had already been seized with panic; the brand image was seriously threatened, store values were plummeting. What was he to say at the press conference?

© 2000 John Wiley & Sons, Ltd.
Understanding Marketing: A European Casebook edited by Celia Phillips, Ad Pruyn and Marie-Paule Kestemont.

Introduction

It is difficult at first sight to classify this case which does not, strictly speaking, fall in European marketing. It deals with crisis management (the "people" section) from the point of view of communication and ethics and short-term rebranding.

Perhaps the first surprise must be the fact that Perrier water spent the first half of the twentieth century under British management with an international market mainly in the British colonies. However, by the time our story begins, the product is, once more, definitely French, and has a flourishing and growing clientele in the United States of America. Readers are thus able to look at the problems of a European product in a US market (as opposed to the Coca-Cola PET Case 9, which looks at the story the other way round!).

Questions focus on what a responsible company president should do when a health-threatening fault is found in a major product in his company. The questions whose answers will affect his decisions are carefully put:

- Is the risk to health great?
- Are rivals playing a role?
- What has caused this?

but above all

- How can the company respond to mounting hysteria in the market place?

Issues of ethics, international marketing and advertising policy are raised for discussion and the slight hint of paranoia – "Some sectors of the economy . . . would welcome any opportunity to attack Fortress Europe" – may merit more serious thought on protectionism and the present marketing constraints between Europe and the USA!

KEYWORDS

Marketing environment, crisis management, ethics, corporate image.

Case

MINERAL WATER WITH MORE THAN 2000 YEARS OF HISTORY

Although its water was first bottled in 1863, the spring at Vergèze – from which all Perrier water now comes – was known even in Roman times. Located near Nimes in southern France, it was only a few hundred yards from Via Minuta, the road between Rome and Spain. Among the traces of the Romans' passing, archaeologists had discovered a stone basin and numerous Roman coins and medals in the area around the spring. According to legend, Hannibal stopped here with his troops, en route to Carthage after defeating the Romans in the year 218 BC.

After a long and varied history, the spring, originally known as Les Bouillens (which translates roughly as "boiling waters") began to be used for commercial purposes. On 23 June 1863, Emperor Napoleon III granted the *Societé de l'Etablissement Thermal des Eaux Minerales de Vergèze* rights to commercialize the spring, and a spa and hotel were built. Bottling also got underway. The company had a number of economic problems during its first years of existence.

In 1903 Les Bouillens was purchased by Sir John Harmsworth, an English aristocrat who renamed the company *Compagnie de la Source Perrier* as a tribute to Dr Louis Perrier, who had headed the company's turnaround during the last decade of the nineteenth century. Under Harmsworth's direction, Perrier went international, exporting mainly to the British colonies where water was either scarce or contaminated. In 1914 production amounted to two million bottles a year. By 1922 it had increased to five million (3.7 million of which were exported) and by 1933 it was up to 18.2 million (8.4 million of which were exported).

Harmsworth died and by the end of the Second World War the company was about to close. Harmsworth's heirs decided to sell to the Levens, a family of French bankers, who named Gustave Leven the company president. A visionary who foresaw changes in European eating and drinking habits, Leven was considered a marketing genius, leading the company as it expanded into more than 100 countries, registering total sales of more than $3 billion dollars (2.84 billion Euros) a year.

Without a doubt, one of Leven's greatest contributions to Perrier was his insistence that the company invest heavily in promotion and advertising, transmitting a creative message that reflected Perrier's image as a dynamic company.

NATURALLY CARBONATED WATER

A number of geological studies trace the formation of the Perrier spring back to the Cretaceous period. For more than 130 million years, rainwater has filtered through limestone, sand and gravel deposits, acquiring the different minerals – calcium, magnesium and bicarbonate – which give Perrier its distinctive taste.

One of Perrier water's most distinguishing features is the fact that it is naturally carbonated as the result of volcanic activity in the subsoil. Originally, the natural gas met and mingled with spring water underground and rose at a constant pressure and temperature (60°F; 15.5°C) at the source. However, by the end of the nineteenth century, increased production and the need to ensure consistent quality caused Perrier to begin drawing the water and the carbonated gas separately, and from different depths within the same geological formation, combining them in the bottling plant after having previously filtered the gas in order to eliminate impurities.

PERRIER IN THE USA

Although Perrier has been available in the US market since the beginning of the twentieth century, sales did not really take off until the late 1970s and early 1980s with the arrival of the health and fitness craze in that country. Perrier became the beverage of choice for yuppies and the brand became generic: people asked for Perrier whenever they wanted mineral water. As Ken Roman, former president of Ogilvy & Mather, put it, "You drink Perrier for its image, not its taste".

With billings of over $160 million in 1989 (in a $2.6-billion market) and a growth of 1% over the previous year, Perrier's position in the US market is good. Sales by volume of 93 million litres ranked it first among imported mineral waters, far ahead of the second-running Evian, whose 1989 sales amounted to 69 million litres (and whose

194% increase over the previous year demonstrates the buoyancy of the market for mineral water products).

FOOD AND DRUG ADMINISTRATION TESTS REVEAL EXCESS BENZENE CONTENT

At the end of January 1990, a routine test made in a North Carolina laboratory revealed an excess of benzene in a few bottles of Perrier. Subsequent analyses by the Food and Drug Administration (FDA) confirmed that 13 bottles of Perrier contained 12.3 to 19.9 parts per million of benzene, when the normal limit permitted by the FDA was only 5 per million. Benzene is a chemical product commonly used in paint manufacturing. A product of naturally carbonated gas, it is also a carcinogenic substance.

The FDA was quick to announce that the contaminated Perrier water would not immediately endanger consumer health. Nor, according to experts, was the long-term danger important because intake of one litre of contaminated water per day for 15 years would increase the risk of cancer from this source to one in a million, 50 times less than the risk run by a non-smoker who inhales smoke from a cigarette 3 metres away. However, such statistics are useless in a panic.

Although the danger was by no means great, the media played up the story and hysteria spread from New York to San Francisco. The news immediately spread to Europe and a few hours later the price of Perrier shares had registered a 12% drop on the Paris Stock Exchange.

PERRIER'S REACTION

A first, but thoroughly unfounded, suspicion was that the Perrier water might have been tampered with in the company warehouses or while it was being distributed in the USA and Canada.

Another theory that started taking shape in some parts of the company was that the FDA was perhaps not totally unbiased. After all, Perrier had a lot of competitors – among them Coca-Cola, Phillip Morris and Cadbury Schweppes – whose powerful lobbies could put considerable pressure on the US government. The fact that the

FDA had issued reports about the benzene discovery while simultaneously underplaying them could be taken as an indication that the FDA's actions had not been entirely on the up-and-up. Some Perrier executives suggested simply ignoring the FDA reports while others advocated fighting back, accusing the government of employing questionable protectionist tactics. 1992 and the Single European Market were just around the corner. Some sectors of the US economy viewed this as a threat and would welcome any opportunity to attack Fortress Europe.

A spokesman for the firm subsequently observed that contamination could have been caused by human error. An employee might have mistakenly used a solution containing benzene when removing grease from the machinery in one of Perrier's bottling plants. However, this seemed highly unlikely in view of the fact that the bottling plants seldom, if ever, used toxic chemical products to clean their machines, precisely in order to avoid contamination.

Another possible cause of the problem might have been that the benzene produced by the naturally carbonated gas had not been totally removed in the filtering process. However, the company would have to decide whether or not it was advisable to offer the media a third explanation of the possible causes of the problem.

The truth is that Perrier's consumers had already been seized by panic, the brand image was seriously threatened, the company's share values were plummeting and Gustave Leven was about to face the press at a time when all the media were waiting to see what stand Perrier would take.

Questions

1. What are Perrier's alternative strategies?
2. What are their advantages and drawbacks?
3. If you were in Leven's place, what decision would you make?

9

Coca-Cola: market launch of a new "green" packaging system

Frank Habann, Hans Hüttemann and Richard Köhler

Case	Packaging strategy
Main focus	Environmental
Subsidiary focus	Advertising
Scene	Germany, worldwide
Players	Government regulations, PET bottles, consumers
Product	Soft drinks

Summary

Coca-Cola is introducing a new refillable PET bottle in order to open up new, ecologically sensitive market segments. Will this marketing launch achieve growth in the soft drinks sector? What central marketing decisions need to be made?

© 2000 John Wiley & Sons, Ltd.
Understanding Marketing: A European Casebook edited by Celia Phillips,
Ad Pruyn and Marie-Paule Kestemont.

Introduction

Case 9 takes readers through the development of a new packaging system for an international brand in a particular country. It introduces us to a fairly complicated political and environmental world. The background is the late 1980s and 1990s first in the Federal Republic of Germany, and later in the greatly enlarged consumer market of the new reunified Germany.

In Germany over the period, environmental issues have become increasingly important to consumers in general, and in particular the importance of bio-friendly packaging in the soft drinks industry.

The authors describe changes in Coca-Cola's packaging methods worldwide – the use of cans, increasingly regarded as ecologically unfriendly, and the new technology of packaging using polyethylene terephthalate (PET) rather than glass. The picture then shifts to Germany where concerns centre on a need to increase sales in a saturated market. One known strategy for doing this with soft drinks is to produce larger packs – and the light new bottles facilitate such a plan. The current packaging systems and their target consumer groups are introduced and the importance of other parts of the marketing system once the decision to introduce a reusable PET bottle had been made spelled out. Likely challenges to distribution, sales and advertising are discussed and finally the story of the two-year test marketing and eventual nationwide launch is told.

The figures presented are detailed, clear and interesting and lead to questions on possible packaging and advertising strategies. Readers may feel on seeing them that Coca-Cola were determined at some points to introduce bottles in the new material against all the odds!

KEYWORDS

Environmentally oriented marketing, innovative packaging strategy, line extension, cannibalization, trade marketing.

Case

In its 112-year history, the Coca-Cola Company of Atlanta has developed into the world's foremost manufacturer of soft drinks. Its turnover in 1997 reached $18.9 billion (roughly 17.9 billion Euros). The company currently sells one billion bottles or cans of their soft drinks every day worldwide.

There can be little doubt that *product packaging* makes a major contribution to this global success, and that it is a core element of Coca-Cola's marketing strategy. From the outset, the unmistakable "contour" bottle developed in 1915 differentiated Coca-Cola from similar products and established it internationally. Over the years, the company has remained a trendsetter in packaging innovations in the soft drinks sector.

In the 1960s, the metal Coca-Cola can led the breakthrough in the use of such products in packaging systems. It led, however, to a backlash in countries where consumers were concerned with environmental issues and media criticism.

By the 1970s, Coca-Cola in the USA had developed the material polyethylene terephthalate (PET) for packaging. This plastic is characterized primarily by its strength, low weight and environmental compatibility. When non-returnable PET bottles were introduced to European markets in the 1980s they were highly successful. Once again, however, a non-return packaging concept such as this, particularly in such a large-volume packaging sector, further blemished Coca-Cola's image with environmentalists. Refillable bottles were needed.

This case study focuses on the goals of the nationwide launch in 1990 of the 1.5 litre refillable PET bottle in the Federal Republic of Germany, as well as the accompanying marketing decisions. It provides an illustration of how an innovation can be assisted in making a breakthrough on the market by focusing marketing activities on the packaging. In addition to the core brand Coke, other brands such as Coke Light, Fanta, Sprite and Bonaqa table water are now also available in the 1.5-litre refillable PET bottle in Germany. This new launch by Coca-Cola Germany has been their most successful to date.

The background to this move is interesting, and has been driven throughout by increasing pressure from the German public about environmental issues, their critical attitude to Coca-Cola's packaging policies and 1980s legislation. For details of this legislation, see the Appendix at the end of this chapter.

The company, which had already introduced the ecologically controversial metal can in its packaging, followed this with a 2-litre non-returnable PET bottle in the mid 1980s and, despite opposition to this, considered introducing a non-deposit 1.5-litre PET bottle as late as 1988.

A 1987 market research study (Essen and Trinken 1987, quoted in Meffert and Kirchgeorg, 1998) shows the importance of environment and eco-friendly packaging to German consumers of non-alcoholic beverages. Eighteen per cent of the consumers studied from the Federal Republic were members of the segment "biologically and ecologically aware consumers"; 32% of the members of this segment said they "take notice of eco-friendly packaging".

At the end of 1988 the Federal German Government imposed a compulsory deposit for drinks in plastic bottles. As a result, Coca-Cola subsequently withdrew its PET non-returnable bottles from the German market at the start of 1989.

Coca-Cola had to think again! Experience with the 2-litre bottle had already shown them that the new packaging material PET was liked by customers. They were happy with both the size of the bottle and the deposit-return system. In fact, even when non-returnable bottles had been used in packaging, Coca-Cola had continued to develop their technology with the refillable bottle. By 1990 a technically refined product was available. A *central goal* of introducing the eco-friendly 1.5-litre refillable PET bottle was to attain an increase in sales through the new packaging system. Forty-five per cent of the company's turnover was still packaged in 1-litre glass bottles and the new refillable bottle aimed to supplement this. It was hoped to boost sales after a period of low growth.

Clearly Coca-Cola had to aim to open up the *environment-oriented market segment* for Coca-Cola found by the researchers. It was known that this target group had a particularly strong thirst for information. This target group had to be presented with, and mobilized by, appropriate evidence.

In addition to opening up this new market segment, the company also expected additional growth stimulus through an *increase in the consumption intensity* per consumer. It was hoped that this would be encouraged because of the low weight of the bottle ("1.5 litres in just 110 grams of packaging") and the associated convenience benefits when shopping and when returning empty bottles. Figure 9.1 shows the advertisements which aimed to communicate these ideas.

FIGURE 9.1   (a) "New. The low weight refillable bottle. *Lightweight.* The 1.5 l refillable PET bottle weighs about 100 grams when empty." (b) "New. The lightweight refillable bottle. *Unbreakable.* The 1.5 l refillable PET bottle is virtually unbreakable." Source: Coca-Cola advertising campaign.

The company expected that the larger volume of the 1.5-litre PET bottle in comparison with the 1-litre glass bottle and the targeted bulk retail in "combi-crates" would achieve a higher level of household stock. This in turn would increase the level of consumption overall. This assumption was based on Coca-Cola's experience in other saturated national markets showing that growth stimulus in the case of soft drinks can most realistically be yielded by increasing the size of the packaging.

With the marketing concept for the 1.5-litre refillable PET bottle focusing on the packaging, great importance was being placed on a component of the product policy that frequently plays a subordinate role during a market launch in the consumer goods sector. Now the design of the other marketing instruments had to be matched to the new packaging.

- *Logistical challenges to distribution policy.* It was expected that the new packaging would yield a reduction in transport and storage costs in comparison with the 1-litre glass bottle because of its low weight and higher content. However, the new form of packaging also called for the use of new bottling technology (the existing bottling plants could only be partially refitted for the new refillable PET technology). Furthermore, adequate stocks of new empty bottles and empty crates had to be made available. Thus, an excessively hasty market penetration would have gone hand-in-hand with the risk of supply bottlenecks.

- *The sales dimension.* This was less difficult. Coca-Cola Germany was able to fall back on its existing sales channels. Its partners in the foodstuffs retail trade, in particular, were quickly convinced of the advantages of the new packaging system. Attention was drawn in this context to the greater retail-space turnover attainable, the low handling costs and the avoidance of bottles breaking in shops and stores. What was more, it would be possible to use Germany's existing deposit-return infrastructure (used with glass bottles) for redistribution of the new PET bottles. The convenience benefits for the consumers, including the simplified return of empty bottles, were another convincing argument for the retailers.
- *Communication policy and the establishment of awareness.* Here it was important to achieve a high degree of awareness of the new bottle and to clearly illustrate its advantages as quickly as possible. In particular, Coca-Cola's challenge was to correct the association chains widespread among consumers of "glass = refillable = eco-friendly" and "plastic = non-returnable = environmentally harmful". Consumers had to be convinced that the refillable PET bottle was environmentally friendly. It was very important to design the advertising statement for the new packaging in such a way that it did not encourage consumers to use interim substitutes before the new refillable 1.5-litre PET was fully launched (they wished to avoid cannibalization). Table 9.1 shows the significant market segments and consumption situations targeted by a the various forms of packaging in the Coca-Cola range.

The market launch of the 1.5-litre refillable PET bottle in Germany was preceded by a market test over several years in the Cologne region. Its aim was to gather technological experience in the field of refillable PET technology in addition to the reaction of consumers and retailers. Thus, for example, the bottle filling and scrubbing technology and properties of the materials used in the new packaging system were tested successfully. Coca-Cola convinced licensees that the new bottling plants were reliable. This market test yielded very encouraging results about the return of bottles. The return rate for the 1.5-litre refillable PET bottles amounted to more

TABLE 9.1   Packaging and market segments – consumption situation, Coca-Cola Germany, 1990s

Form of packaging (volume in litres)	Market segment/consumption situation
0.2 l glass refillable	Superior catering
0.33 l glass refillable	General outdoor consumption; vending machines
0.5 l glass refillable	Small storage size for households; partly also for outdoor consumption
1.0 l glass refillable	Storage size for environmentally oriented households
1.5 l PET refillable	*Clearly the 1.5 PET refillable should aim at the new storage size for households, but what other segments might it fill?*
0.15 l can	Outdoor consumption; distributed to airlines only
0.33 l can	Outdoor consumption for sport and travel; also for household storage
0.5 l can	Packaging alternative to 0.33 l can for "serious thirst"
0.33 l glass non-return	Outdoor consumption; practical thanks to screw-top
0.5 l glass non-return	Outdoor consumption; primarily for "serious thirst"
1.0 l glass non-return	Storage size for households

Source: Coca-Cola, in-house.

than 90%, which slightly surpassed the rate for the traditional 1-litre glass bottle.

The market test had interesting implications for marketing activity and sales development. Results on this informed the eventual nationwide launch of the new package.

Initial sales of the new product in the first few months of the test were disappointing. This could be partly explained by the fact that the packaging system was only used for the core product, Coca-Cola, and advertising not very fully launched. But even after all the brands manufactured by Coca-Cola began to use the new packaging system several months after the start of the test, and despite a marked increase in the number of outlets participating in the test market, sales still failed to improve. What should Coca-Cola do now?

Halfway through the test there was a massive increase in promotion of the new product, primarily through newspaper advertisements and sales-promoting activities. At the same time, the number of participating retail outlets was further increased. In addition, the price of the new bottle (which had previously been 10% higher by volume than the 1-litre glass bottle) was lowered to an equivalent level. This combination of focused advertising, the increase in

participating retail outlets and reduction in prices led to a clear
upswing in demand. Figure 9.2 gives the data.

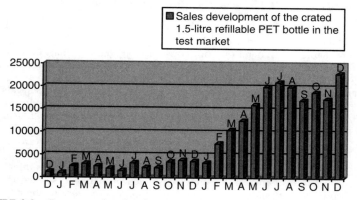

FIGURE 9.2   German sales development of the crated 1.5-litre refillable PET bottle
in the test market over a two-year test period. Source: Coca-Cola, in-house.

In the middle of the second test year there was a bottleneck in the
supply of the new bottles, and Coca-Cola was temporarily unable to
cover demand for a short period of time. This led to a temporary
decline in turnover.

In fact, while sales of the new bottle did well, there was also a
significant boost in Coca-Cola's deposit-return business and the
1-litre glass bottle was not clearly superseded. Nevertheless, on its
introduction *nationwide*, the 1.5-litre refillable PET bottle developed
into an important pillar of sales for Coca-Cola Germany. By 1997,
share of the company's sales volume amounted to around 33% This,
combined with the 1995/96 nationwide launch of the 1-litre refillable
PET bottle, led to the virtual death of the 1-litre deposit-return glass
bottle.

The transformation of the packaging strategy from glass to PET in
the deposit-return sector can thus be regarded as successfully implemented from a commercial standpoint. Figures show that sales of
refillables within the product programme for Coca-Cola Germany
rose from 63.1% in 1990 to 75.8% in 1997.

That the packaging strategy can also be regarded as successful in a
non-commercial context is shown by the fact that the refillable
PET bottle had won five prizes for environmental and innovation

packaging by 1995. Coca-Cola thus appears to be on the right course in terms of ecological acceptance and an environmentally oriented self-image.

Questions

1. What were the principal goals of Coca-Cola Germany's market launch of the 1.5-litre refillable PET packaging unit in Germany?
2. Justify the *gradual* introduction of the new packaging system following the market test.
3. What arguments would you employ in order to induce retailers to adopt the 1.5-litre refillable bottle, thus expanding their range?
4. Analyse the advertisements shown in Figures 9.1(a) and (b) for the introduction of the 1.5-litre refillable PET bottle as regards their expressive content.

Acknowledgements

The authors would like to thank Coca-Cola company for their kind support.

References and further reading

Boesch, M. (1989) Gesamtsystem Verpackung – Grundlage für optimale, integrierte Verpackungsentscheidungen (Packaging as an overall system – the basis for optimum, integrated packaging decisions). St Gallen: Thesis.

Hopfenbeck, W. (1994) *Umweltorientiertes Management und Marketing: Konzepte – Instrumente – Praxisbeispiele (Environmentally Oriented Management and Marketing – Concepts – Instruments – Practical Examples)*, 3rd edn. Landsberg/Lech: Moderne Industrie.

Kaluza, B. (ed.) (1997) *Unternehmung und Umwelt (Business and the Environment)*, 2nd edn. Hamburg: S + W Steuer- und Wirtschaftsverlag.

Kirchgeorg, M. (1990) *Ökologieorientiertes Unternehmensverhalten (Eco-Oriented Corporate Behaviour)*. Wiesbaden: Gabler.

Meffert, H. and Kirchgeorg, M. (1998) *Marktorientiertes Umweltmanagement. Konzeption – Strategie – Implementierung mit Praxisfällen (Environmental Management. Conception – Strategy – Implementation and Practical Cases)*, 3rd edn. Stuttgart: Schäffer-Poeschel.
Peattie, K. (1995) *Environmental Marketing Management: Meeting the Green Challenge*. London: Pitman Publishing.
Welford, R. and Gouldson, A. (1993) *Environmental Management and Business Strategy*. London: Pitman Publishing.

Appendix

LEGISLATION ON PACKAGING IN GERMANY

Two laws have affected Coca-Cola's packaging policy in Germany.

The first, dated 27 August 1986, is on the avoidance and disposal of waste. "Gesetz über die Vermeidung und Entsorgung von Abfällen" can be regarded as the original motivator for introducing the 1.5-litre refillable PET bottle.

It was followed by a decree on compulsory deposits for plastic bottles ("Verordnung über die Rücknahme und Pfanderhebung von Getränkeverpackungen aus Kunststoffen") on 20 December 1988.

10

The Ullman chair: potential for success?

Staffan Hultén

Case	New product
Main focus	Marketing strategy
Subsidiary focus	Technical development, entrepreneurship, distribution
Scene	Sweden
Players	Individual designer, big business
Product	Furniture

Summary

Johan Ullman, inventor and doctor, invented a novel orthopaedic-style office chair in 1984. Originally sold through Ericsson, it was eventually marketed by Design Function AB, a small furniture producer, which went bankrupt in 1993.

The chair had been reasonably successful until the years immediately before bankruptcy. Ullman still has the right to sell to private individuals. How should he now proceed? Should he look for a new manufacturer, or set up his own business?

© 2000 John Wiley & Sons, Ltd.
Understanding Marketing: A European Casebook edited by Celia Phillips,
Ad Pruyn and Marie-Paule Kestemont.

Introduction

This new product case moves us away from the big battalions and international corporations and traces the progress of a man and his idea for an innovative product.

The Ullman chair in both its main forms should be reasonably familiar to readers, perhaps because of its many imitators. It is an excellent example of an idiosyncratic product that may take some selling in the first place – but could take off with the right marketing.

Two particular strands make this case interesting:

- The technical changes which were introduced are carefully described
- The changes in business fortune which occurred and over which Ullman could have no control are also observed from near partnership with a furniture company with 70 stores, to a larger, foreign-owned firm

The perils to the small business are clear, and readers are invited to speculate as to what went wrong, and how Ullman (who still has the rights to private and medical sales) could proceed and make a success of an exciting product.

KEYWORDS

Ergonomic design, entrepreneurship, innovation, marketing strategy.

Case

Johan Ullman – an inventor and doctor – invented a novel office chair in 1984. He became interested in chairs when he worked in an orthopaedic clinic in a town hospital. After some time he developed back and neck problems and when he asked the physiotherapists for help he found their suggestions did not help. They recommended that he sit in an upright position, but he was both unwilling and unable to sit like that – it was too uncomfortable! Instead he started to explore different seating postures in an attempt to solve his problems. He found out that the least pain-provoking posture was when he sat at the edge of a table and let his thighs slope downward with his feet positioned under his behind.

He developed a prototype in 1982–1983 – a stool with a sloping seat. However, testers found it impossible to sit on a forward sloping surface without sliding forward. Undaunted by this setback, Ullman continued to develop more prototypes and got backing from organizations which funded the development of new products. In 1984 he presented an improved model. This prototype had the rear half of the seat flat. Only the front half sloped forward. The new model was launched at a national fair in Stockholm for new products – SKAPA-mässan. Three different models were shown with and without backrest. He was so confident in the new chair that he filed a patent application before publicizing his invention.

Despite its rudimentary design, the chair was a success. People lined up to test the product and many hundred individuals and organizations wanted to order the new chair. Two state agencies in the public health sector showed an interest. Ullman also got a substantial amount of media coverage for the product. In an interview he stated:

> I believe that the reason why people accept my chair is the fact that it is doesn't look so different from a standard office chair. It is only the seat that is different.

Ullman contacted a couple of furniture producers and finally decided to sign a contract with Ericsson's (the telecommunication firm) furniture company in Åtvidaberg. The factory in Åtvidaberg mainly produced office desks. At this time Ericsson was investing heavily in the paper-free office concept and supplied everything from computers to telephones and furniture.

The adaptation of the new chair to Ericsson's furniture production was managed by a product developer at Ericsson. The first product development measure was to provide a backrest for the chair. This was done by putting an Ullman seat on a standard Ericsson chair. In this way the Ullman chair acquired many attributes that became important for the chair – a backrest lever, tilting seat and easily adjustable controls. Ullman had to fight for his ideas such as getting the shape of backrest he wanted. When the new model of the chair was tested it was observed that some people slid off the seat – small women in short skirts were at particular risk! The design of the seat was therefore altered. In particular, the sloping part was shortened. Ullman managed to put his personal touch on the model by styling the backrest and seatpan with octagonal shapes. Mass production began after these changes were incorporated in the design. Two basic designs were offered: an office chair (with or without armrest) and a stool. In addition, Ercisson developed a special design for surgeons (Ullman's colleagues at the hospital) which enabled them to sit and do surgery which previously could be done only in a standing position.

In 1985 the chair was presented to the press under the name "Ullmanstolen" (the Ullman chair). Ericsson and Ullman agreed that while Ericsson would be responsible for sales to offices and industries, Ullman would retain an interest and the right to sell direct to private customers and to the medical and dental sector.

Less than a year later Ericsson sold its furniture factory to Design Funktion AB, a furniture producer with a couple of hundred employees whose majority shareholder was a Norwegian company. This change of ownership had no immediate effect on the cooperation between Ullman and the furniture firm. New models were launched and unsuccessful models gradually withdrawn, including the original stool model which showed disappointing sales figures despite efforts to improve the design.

Two new models were launched in 1987–1998: an executive model and a more stylish office chair with octagonal seat and backrest. The latter became the bestselling Ullman chair. Many minor changes were also made in the designs: new and better tilt mechanisms, improved padding, and the replacement of metal detailing by plastic.

The Ullman chair's main sales outlet was "Ericsson City" – 70 office furniture and computer stores which marketed the furniture from Ericsson's furniture factory. When Ericsson sold the furniture firm the stores continued to cooperate with the new owners. The other sales outlets were Design Funktion's exhibition centres in six Swedish towns; direct contacts between Design Funktion and architects, builders etc.; and Ullman's own company.

The Ullman chair was an unusual product in the Design Funktion's product programme. Its sloping seat made many potential customers unwilling to sit in the chair while other customers found it superior to

TABLE 10.1   Sales development for the Ullman chair in million Swedish krona (Sweden, 1985–1992)

1985	1986	1987	1988	1989	1990	1991	1992
0.5	3.9	3.4	4.1	4.5	5.2	3.8	2.2

Source: in-house.

other chairs in the market. Clearly the chair needed more work to boost sales. Ullman asked Design Funktion to honour its licence agreement and provide this by organizing education days for the sales force and important customers about the principles of the chair. This was only done on three occasions. Ullman participated and explained his ideas and demonstrated the chair. Design Funktion printed brochures on the Ullman chair in which Ullman explained his ideas about the importance of variation and balanced sitting. The chair was marketed both as a stand-alone product and in conjunction with other office furniture marketed by Design Funktion.

The Ullman chair continued to get positive media coverage. Most articles dealt both with the Ullman chair and Ullman's work as an inventor in general. As time passed, Ullman's chair met competition from other Scandinavian firms which produced office chairs with an explicit ergonomic design. The most prominent rival was Stokke, a Norwegian firm with an extensive product programme of wooden ergonomic office chairs. In 1990 Stokke had a turnover of 126 million Norwegian krona (about 15.3 million Euros). Table 10.1 gives data on sales development for the Ullman chair.

Other producers were the Swedish firm RH-form, and the two Norwegian firms Rybo and Håg. The basic idea of many of the Norwegian ergonomic office chairs was that the seated person could rest his back by leaning his knee on a support. The RH-form office chairs integrated some ergonomic design features and had an overall unique design but were designwise fairly close to mainstream office chairs.

In 1992 Sweden experienced its worst economic crisis in 50 years and the building of offices and homes was particularly badly hit. This produced severe problems for Design Funktion and the firm rapidly reduced production and the number of employees. These measures were unable to stop the firm from going bankrupt in 1993.

Questions

1. Why was it difficult to expand the market for the Ullman chair?
2. Kotler's *Marketing Management* (1997) lists the German firm Braun's ten principles of good design. They are:
   (i)   Good design is innovative
   (ii)   Good design enhances the usefulness of a product
   (iii)   Good design is aesthetic
   (iv)   Good design displays the logical structure of a product; its form follows its function
   (v)   Good design is unobtrusive
   (vi)   Good design is honest
   (vii)   Good design is enduring
   (viii) Good design is consistent right down to details
   (ix)   Good design is ecologically conscious
   (x)   Good design is minimal design
   To what extent does the Ullman chair live up to these ten principles? Do you think that the chair would have been more accepted in the market place if Ullman had managed to design a chair in exact accordance with these principles?
3. If you were Ullman, how would you now proceed to market your chair? What would be the advantages and disadvantages of (i) looking for a new partner manufacturer and (ii) setting up your own small business making the chairs?

References and further reading

Besanko, D., Dranove, D. and Shanley, M. (1996) *The Economics of Strategy*. New York: Wiley.
Kotler, P. (1997) *Marketing Management*, 9th edn. Englewood Cliffs, NJ: Prentice Hall.

11

The Fair Trade and "Made in Dignity" labels

Marie-Paule Kestemont and Valerie Swaen

Case	Branding
Main focus	Pricing
Subsidiary focus	Ethics, labour policy
Scene	Europe, particularly Belgium, Eire and the UK, and the third world
Players	OXFAM, supermarkets, producer, consumer
Product	Consumer goods

Summary

A partner in the European Fair Trade Association, OXFAM world shops have created their own label "Made in Dignity" for craft and textile products. OXFAM world shops aim at creating and developing brand image customer loyalty, selecting relevant distribution channels, despite the high price of such specific products. The rewards in terms of social engineering are clear, but what of profits? Can this strategy work?

© 2000 John Wiley & Sons, Ltd.
Understanding Marketing: A European Casebook edited by Celia Phillips,
Ad Pruyn and Marie-Paule Kestemont.

Introduction

Case 11 is truly international. It looks at product branding with an emphasis on pricing. The effects of marketing practices on the labour force in
third world countries are connected to the desire of European consumers
for competitively priced products. The writers move on from the usual
conception of OXFAM as a chain of charity used-clothes shops and ask
readers to consider its distribution and marketing policy with new
products.

We are first reminded of the original "Fair Trade" policy of OXFAM
imported goods and their system of distribution through world shops, mail
order and increasingly, supermarket and grocery outlets. "Fair Trade"
products are available in nine European countries, and the organization of
three of them – in Belgium, Eire and the UK – is described in detail.

Sales and price figures are given and a picture of the retail system
presented. Consumer reaction to the "Fair Trade" label is discussed. We are
told that there is reasonably high awareness of "Fair Trade" in all three
countries, and a stated willingness by some consumers in Belgium and the
UK to buy such products. While commercial importers and wholesalers in
Eire are not very interested in "Free Trade" products, we are told that
supermarkets in the UK are experiencing better sales than they expected – at
a mark-up of 5–10% above comparable products (and 25% in the case of
coffee). A UK customer profile is also given.

A moderate success story then, which appears to be gradually taking off
in recent years. What of the "Made in Dignity" label? Can this enhance the
products concerned?

KEYWORDS

Fair trade, brand image, loyalty, positioning, distribution.

Case

In an editorial in the *Wall Street Journal* (9 April 1996), clothing
industry consultant David Birnbam wrote: "For the first time, human
rights concerns could become a major marketing issue and tool for
manufacturers."

FAIR TRADE IN EUROPE

In January 1994, the European Parliament adopted a resolution promoting fairness and solidarity in North–South trade. Measures to strengthen and support the Fair Trade movement and to adopt the Fair Trade principles in policies of the European Union and its member states were recommended.

> Fair Trade supports poor people who face disadvantages, but are working to overcome them through their own efforts. Fair Trade is about giving poor people power: by paying producers a fair price for their work, and by strengthening their hand in trading relationships. Fair Trade means that many of the people who rely on selling crafts and textiles for a living or who produce food items such as tea, coffee, chocolate, and honey now have the chance to work their way out of poverty. (**http://www.oneworld.org/oxfam, 1999**)

The European Fair Trade Association (EFTA) includes 11 Fair Trade organizations (Commerce Equitable, 1995) (trade organizations promoting development towards self-reliance and empowerment through establishing fair trade relations, buying coffee, tea, other commodities, textiles and handicrafts directly from organized producers in Africa, Asia and Latin America) in nine European countries (Austria, Belgium, France, Germany, Italy, the Netherlands, Norway, Switzerland and the UK).

The Fair Trade import organizations buy products which have been manufactured and distributed in a socially responsible way from more than 800 000 producers in the third world. They have a social development objective of guaranteeing a fair price to the producers, which enables them and their families to make an adequate living. Producers must respect the natural and social environment through their production methods and in addition goods must be quality products. Fair Trade organizations also help the producers in product development through education and training, improving the organization and marketing of producers and allowing them to share skills and experience with others.

In Europe, Fair Trade import organizations sell their products through world shops, local groups, exhibitions, campaigns, wholesale and mail-order catalogues. They provide information about the producers and their products by means of booklets accompanying the products, exhibitions and magazines. There are more than 3000 world shops in Europe which involve more than 50 000 voluntary workers in their management. These shops cooperate at local, regional, national and international level with the help of the National Associations.

In fact, Fair Trade is attracting increasing numbers of consumers. One can observe that its extent and impact differ from country to country, depending on the "age" of the national movement: the older the movement, the more impact Fair Trade has in the country. In most European countries, Fair Trade has grown by 10 to 25% per year but there is still a considerable gap between actual and potential turnover. Nevertheless, in all European countries, sizeable consumer groups declare that they are prepared to pay 10 to 20% more for Fair Trade products (Oikos and Martinelli 1995 – work commissioned by EFTA).

FAIR TRADE LABELLING

Consumers in Europe are already accustomed to Fair Trade labelling. Industry and trade are invited to adopt the Fair Trade model by, for instance, putting a number of certified Fair Trade products on the market. Different associations provide Fair Trade labelling or certification with the aim of enlarging the market for fairly traded products. The Fair Trade labelled products are offered to the mainstream market (supermarkets, etc.), and at the same time consumers are given an independent guarantee of Fair Trade standards.

OXFAM'S NETWORK

OXFAM's network of shops is an important actor in the field of Fair Trade. This is particularly the case in Belgium, the UK and Ireland. OXFAM is involved in importing, wholesaling and retailing Fair Trade products which are sold through the world shops and supermarkets. In addition, groceries, such as coffee, are sold through general stores and supermarkets.

The main range of OXFAM products include crafts and food: ceramics, tableware, glassware, baskets, textiles, throws, rugs, coffee, teas, jams, honey, spices, chocolate, cocoa, sugar. They are sold at a price somewhat higher than those of comparable non Fair Trade products.

FAIR TRADE IN BELGIUM

There are three Fair Trade organizations in Belgium: the Magasins du Monde Oxfam (in the Walloon part of the country), the Oxfam Wereldwinkels (in the Flemish part) and the (Dutch) Fair Trade Organisatie, active in the field of wholesaling. Max Havelaar is the Fair Trade mark organization in Belgium used for coffee in supermarkets and in the three Fair Trade organizations. More recently Max Havelaar has begun to sell bananas. The OXFAM world shops employ about 40 people in total and Max Havelaar three (Kremer, 1997).

In all, around 300 world shops, several hundred supermarkets (belonging to the eight major supermarket chains in Belgium) and a few individual grocery stores sell Fair Trade products. In 1994, the total retail turnover for world shops in Wallonia was 1.6 million ECU (Euros). In Flanders it was 6.5 million ECU (Euros).

The main products sold are coffee, wine, honey, textiles, chocolate and nuts. Coffee is the most important product in terms of turnover, with a wholesale value of 1.6 million ECU, followed by wine, which was worth 700 000 ECU in 1993. A steady growth can be observed in Fair Trade in Belgium, in terms of both points of sale and turnover. The growth in turnover of Max Havelaar coffee has been about 10% per year. Retail prices of Fair Trade products are somewhat higher than those of comparable non Fair Trade products, but price differences are said to be smaller than in the other European countries. Coffee is about 15 to 20% more expensive, but handicrafts can be cheaper.

Public awareness of Fair Trade is estimated to range between 60 and 70%, while 17% of the population are willing to buy Fair Trade coffee (Oikos and Martinelli 1995). The most successful world shops seem to be located in medium-sized towns, where people do their day-to-day shopping in a number of different shops. The average customers are women, 20–45 years old, with secondary or higher education, employed in the social sector with an above average income (but often below their level of education). The OXFAM world shops' image is slightly "old fashioned". It has to be improved: product innovation is needed and the sales force has to be dynamized (Mémoire, enquete Belgique 1997).

FAIR TRADE IN IRELAND

The Irish Fair Trade Network (IFTN) is an "umbrella" organization functioning as a network for the distribution of Fair Trade products and for the promotion of educational campaigns among all groups involved in development aid and education. In Ireland, Tradeireann is the national organization that concentrates on importing, wholesaling and retailing Fair Trade products. In Northern Ireland, two organizations are active: Trocaire and War on Want. In addition, there are four wholesale organizations that import Fair Trade products from alternative trading organizations in the UK. The retail network includes the OXFAM shops, a few Third World Shops and a number of supermarkets and health food shops – all in all some 60 points of sale. Another retail channel is the mail-order catalogue of Trocaire, mainly distributed in Northern Ireland.

Apart from this, most commercial importers and wholesalers show little interest in Fair Trade. Thus lack of response may derive from lack of knowledge and awareness about Fair Trade. It is not possible to quantify consumer reaction because market research has not been carried out at a national level. A local survey, however (in-house information), indicates that the average consumer is cost-conscious, committed and increasingly interested in development and equity issues. Generally speaking, the products are comparatively expensive since most of them are imported via the UK.

FAIR TRADE IN THE UNITED KINGDOM

Seven importers and five wholesalers deal with Fair Trade. These are Traidcraft, OXFAM Trading, Twin Trading, Equal Exchange, Tearcraft, Shared Earth and Bishopston Trading. There are about 3000 points of sale, including independent shops.

OXFAM, Shared Earth and Bishopston Trading have their own shops. The retail network then consists of world shops, chains of Fair

Trade stores (mainly the 625 OXFAM shops) and some mail-order catalogues. The sector employs about 650 people (excluding the world shops, which are run by around 30 000 voluntary workers). One trademark, the Fairtrade Mark, is operated by the Fairtrade Foundation for the labelling of coffee, teas and chocolate. Fairtrade Mark products are available from the major supermarket chains and from a range of health food shops, smaller stores and independent retailers, totalling over 1000 points of sale.

Wholesale and retail turnover are 3.2 and 5 million ECU respectively for Traidcraft, and 11.3 and 12.7 million ECU respectively for OXFAM Trading. Wholesale and retail turnover for products with a Fairtrade brand name generated a wholesale turnover of 4.8 million ECU in 1994 and expect a turnover of 7.7 million ECU in 1995.

Marketing surveys have indicated that 85% of respondents said they would like to see fairly traded products in their supermarket. Forty per cent were aware of the availability of Fair Trade products in supermarkets. Sixty-eight per cent of the public would be willing to pay a higher price for fair trade products (Oikos and Martinelli 1995).

Health food wholesalers have welcomed the introduction of Fair Trade branded products and in the supermarkets; the products have sold better than was originally expected. In fact, supermarkets are now prepared to introduce new products which carry the Fair Trade label. In general current products sell at 5 to 10% higher than non Fair Trade competitors, but coffee may be up to 25% higher.

Goods traded are coffee, tea, chocolate, other food products, clothing, fashion goods, handicrafts, gifts, textiles, beverages, recycled paper and greeting cards. On the whole, all alternative trade importers have achieved major improvements in design, quality and presentation of the products in the past few years. Consumers still expect the quality of Fair Trade products to be lower than it actually is nowadays. The product range is improving, although changes in both availability and product innovation are hampered by supply and design constraints. World shops tend to be poorly located and under-resourced but are said to be improving.

Traidcraft's customers are mostly women, aged between 25 and 55, with above average incomes. They are often employed in the social sector. The customers of the OXFAM shops are more diverse and the consumer's perception of these shops could be of "shops dedicated for helping poor countries only, not so much active, aiming at marketing fairly traded products from overseas".

Traidcraft has been able to grow by increasing its range of products and value of sales on an existing market. OXFAM Trading mainly sells handicrafts (87%), with coffee as the main food product. OXFAM reports no further growth in turnover, product range or points of sale.

OXFAM AND THE "MADE IN DIGNITY" LABEL

OXFAM has also introduced a "Made in Dignity" label for textile and craft products. OXFAM aims to intensify support for Fair Trade labels in Europe and to enlarge the market for fairly traded products. A recent "Made in Dignity" campaign focused on labour conditions in the garment industry and the exploitation of workers.

By buying "Made in Dignity" products, the consumer encourages those producers who respect the environment and their workers, by giving them fair working conditions and payment. Social and environmental issues are the core "conditions" for a "Made in Dignity" label.

This is a first attempt at defocalizing labour (bringing local labour conditions more into line with international standards) and giving third world brands a value that is comparable to Western ones. It is also a way of protecting children. "Made in Dignity" can be regarded as a first step towards delocalization as third world labour can be properly recognized and rewarded. Recognition by European and third world countries of "Made in Dignity" products should also lead to increasing protection of children in the workplace through government legislation or trade union rules.

"Made in Dignity" products have only been available in the Belgian world shops or in the Belgian catalogue up till now. But OXFAM aims to promote this label in other countries through its specific retail channels, or in association with other Fair Trade networks, or through usual distribution channels.

Consumers generally are not able to choose between different brands (in a supermarket) in terms of fair trade criteria: they know nothing about the conditions in which the goods they buy were manufactured. Moreover, the relatively higher price of such products constitutes an obstacle to demand in the usual distribution channels. For a variety of reasons – the price of the products, the profile of the non Fair Trade consumer and the multiplicity of brands and substitute products in the usual distribution channels – the promotion of Fair Trade products and of the "Made in Dignity" label is a challenge for OXFAM.

Questions

1. Is the "Made in Dignity" labelling policy of OXFAM a relevant issue for Fair Trade?
2. What kind of distribution channel(s) should OXFAM select for developing the brand image and the customer's loyalty (world shops, supermarkets, individual stores)? What are the respective advantages/disadvantages?
3. How might you publicize "Made in Dignity" products?
4. How would you make such products as competitive and attractive as the non Fair Trade products?

References and further reading

Barrett Brown, M. (1995) *Fair Trade: Reforms and Realities in the International Trading System*. ZED Books.
Caste, B. (1992) *The Trade Trap: Poverty and the Global Commodity Market*. Oxfam Publishing.
Commerce Equitable (1995) European Fair Trade Association, Memento.
Editorial (1996) *Wall Street Journal*, April 9.
Kremer, P. (1997) Etude d'image des magasins du Monde Oxfam. Louvain-la-Neuve (unpublished student thesis).
Le Quesne, C. (1996) *Reforming World Trade: The Social and Environmental Priorities*. Oxfam Insight.
Morelle, D. (1995) Compagne "Made in Dignity: les habits de misere". *Demain le Monde* no. 6.
Oikos, E. and Martinelli, E. (1995) *An EFTA Survey of Fair Trade in Europe*, May 1995.
Watkins, K. (1998) *Economic Growth with Equity*. Oxfam Insight.

12

Petrobank: a new competitor in the market place?

Robert Kozielski

Case	Strategic marketing
Main focus	Banking services, home banking
Subsidiary focus	Technological changes, competition
Scene	Poland, Europe-wide
Players	Home bank, international finance, business customers
Product	Banking services

Summary

The analysis of the case concentrates on questions related to marketing activity in the Polish banking sector. The relationship between current trends in globalization and concentration and consequence possibilities of competition on the international market are examined. Analysis focuses on the possibility of introducing a new banking product on to the market and reaching through it a stronger competitive position, in comparison with foreign banks entering the Polish market. In addition to raising marketing questions related to the introduction of the product in the market, the analysis also deals with aspects of global competition. In particular, the case aims to initiate a discussion on the peculiarity of the Polish banking sector and its current transformations in the light of changes in the banking business in the European Union. Against this background the case analyses problems related to the market enterprises of a particular Polish bank and looks at the influence of macro- and micro-environmental factors on the bank's marketing activity.

© 2000 John Wiley & Sons, Ltd.
Understanding Marketing: A European Casebook edited by Celia Phillips, Ad Pruyn and Marie-Paule Kestemont.

Introduction

This strategic marketing case gives us the opportunity to think about banking services in two ways:

- As a challenge to develop the market for banking products in a relatively immature market
- As a case on the introduction of "home banking" and its competitive advantages

It offers its users the possibility of looking at some established theoretical ideas in marketing in a relatively unfamiliar environment.

Readers are taken through different aspects of the developing banking sector in Poland from the point of view of both companies and individual consumers. Former problems due to lack of confidence in the system and a shortage of ready money to invest are explained. Comparative figures with other EU countries are given which help put the landscape in focus – a different one from the "normal" world of bank machines on every corner known to many readers. The fact that the Polish banking system is very open to mergers and takeovers is emphasized and its implications opened for discussion.

Once the scene is set, Petrobank SA is introduced. Beginning in 1990 as the "Credit Company of Lódź", by 1996 it had been renamed, issued shares and, almost inevitably, been taken over by a large Korean capital group.

Up to this point, the bank had concentrated on building its relationship with active and expanding Polish businesses. It had opened new branches throughout Poland and was in a strong position at a national level. This new influx of money, however, meant that the bank felt it was time to compete – to gain a larger share of the Polish market and become a player in the international market. "Home banking" is one of the ways Petrobank has chosen to achieve this.

Readers from EU and American countries are invited to imagine themselves in a financial world some way from their own – but which is rapidly taking on our characteristics – and work out how the marketing theories they have been taught apply in these circumstances.

KEYWORDS

Marketing, international marketing, marketing in banking sector.

Case

CHARACTERISTICS OF THE POLISH BANK SERVICE MARKET

Many reasons are given by banking experts for the fact that Polish banks appear unprepared to contribute substantially to business or national development or to compete in an effective manner with foreign banks (Wiśniewska 1998). The main factors are

- A weak and divided bank system
- The limited scope of financial services offered by banks
- Lengthy operational procedures
- Insufficient knowledge of, or competence, in banking procedures

Evidence of such weaknesses are illustrated by basic indices which give a picture of the Polish banking sector. In 1997, for example, its assets were 53% of gross national product (i.e. a third of that for Germany and a quarter of that in France). The underlying reasons for this stem from years of socialist economics and the current changes which are taking place.

In fact the former Polish People's Republic had no banking market at all. There was no competition between financial institutions and so the possibilities of utilizing various bank services were limited. The introduction of market economy principles has contributed to the partial opening of banks to customers and to the gradual extension of services, which should lead to positive developments. That is the principle and it seems to explain the high appreciation of banks by Polish people six years after the market transformation process began. This is surprising given that half (54%) of the Polish population still do not utilize the services of any bank and that 84% of those who do are customers of the one bank alone. Figures from the Institute of Opinion and Market Research (1996) show that over 13 million adult Poles do not use bank services. The reasons for this are many and various:

- Lack of banking traditions
- The limited range of financial services offered

- The low financial credibility of the banks, shortage of lending money to use for investments or payment by instalments.

Poland's transition from central planning to a market economy has also involved specific processes of adaptation in the activities of Polish banks. The most obvious sign of these transformations is the increasing range of financial services offered by the banks in order to improve their competitiveness. Although banks operating in the domestic market offer different services, some services are common to all. These include:

- Saving and clearing accounts
- Bank account credits
- Consumer's credits
- Credits for the purchase of vehicles
- Short-, medium- and long-term market investments
- Credit on securities
- Credit on mortgage or economic credits

Some banks, however, provide additional services such as computerized credit cards or so-called "home banking". The services on offer from such banks differ not only in their scope but also in the terms of purchase.

Uptake is limited. In the retail market, for example, investments and bank credits are most frequently required. Gradually the new services are being taken up. In 1996, for example, savings went up by 12.1% for the first two months compared with an increase of 47.6% for the whole of 1995 (National Bank of Poland 1996). In addition, the Industrial-Commercial Bank saw customers' deposits in Polish currency increase within a year from zl.1567 million (about 392.2 million Euros) to zl.2331 million, i.e. by 48.8%. In addition, there has been an increase in the size of saving and clearing accounts of about 150% over 1995–1996. The explanation for this rapid rise usually centres on the fact that the deposit rate for the Polish zloty is more advantageous than for foreign currency accounts and the value of the dollar on the world market has been decreasing over the period. It seems, however, that the main reasons for this state of affairs lie in rising confidence in Polish currency coupled with greater financial confidence among wider groups of Polish society.

The average amount of financial liability per person in Poland is not heavy by Western standards. The average Polish adult owes the equivalent of about $120 to the bank, that is about half the average monthly wage. This compares with a debit equivalent to annual earnings in countries with a developed market economy

Up to the end of 1994 nearly all Poles were afraid to make purchases using bank credit. A real increase in value of the credits given began in 1995, when they rose by 11% compared with the preceding year. Individual customer liabilities exceeded zl.5.6 billion and bank debits showed an increase of 67.5% over 1994. The first half-year of 1996 brought still better results: the amount of loans raised in that period increased by 42% and by a further 2.2% in the first ten days of July. The following years brought and will continue to bring further increases. Therefore the indices representing the strength of the Polish banking business on the one hand highlight the weakness of this economic sector but on the other reflect its development possibilities. Forecasts such as these from the National Bank of Poland have led to a growing engagement of foreign banks in the Polish banking business. For example, German banking establishments now control about 15% of Polish bank capital, American institutions 11.5% and the Netherlands around 7.5% (Kowalik 1998).

THE POLISH BANKING SECTOR IN THE LIGHT OF MARKET GLOBALIZATION

The world banking business has been undergoing quantitative and qualitative transformations since the mid 1980s which affect many aspects of bank operations. As integration with the European Union approaches, it is necessary to examine the consequences of these changes in the Polish financial system on world markets and the operating of Polish banks. The main reason for the changes which have so far been implemented in the Polish banking system is to create necessary competitiveness to deal with the new global bank system. The changes in question involve processes which can also be seen in the financial establishments of well-developed economies. The most important of these are:

- The privatization of the banking system and its consolidation
- Changes related to banking technology (in particular the influence of computerization on bank operations).

In order to look at the scope of privatization it is necessary to refer to the role of foreign capital in the banking business of EU countries. At the beginning of the 1990s the proportion of national banks compared with foreign banks in the total assets of the banking sector amounted to 87% in Portugal and 42% in France, for example, compared with 47% for Poland. From these data it appears that the share of the Bank of Poland in the banking system is not different from the standard solutions adopted in EU countries. It is worth noting, however, that the Polish situation is unusual in the extent to which Polish banks are undercapitalized (the total amount of their own funds in the Polish banking system is several times lower than the capital in each of the 15 largest European banks): the most rapid way of raising capital is by drawing on foreign investors. For this reason it seems likely that future years will see increasing takeovers of Polish banks by international establishments (Bandyk 1998).

Another pronounced tendency seen in Poland is the process of consolidation in the financial market and the whole economy alike, which mirrors changes in the economic systems of most developed countries. Most recent mergers have involved establishments such as Boeing and McDonnell Douglas, AT&T and TCI, and Chrysler and Daimler Benz. Consolidating tendencies in the financial sector have also become more intense worldwide. As a result, great conglomerates, combining both banks and assurance companies, have been born. The dynamics of these changes are shown in Table 12.1. In 1985 there were only 52 mergers and takeovers in the EU banking sector; by 1996 such amalgamations were already over the 400 mark.

The aim of such a process of consolidation is to reach effects of scale and synergy which lead to increased competitiveness in the market. In the Polish market, we expect the process of such consolidation to be abrupt because of the atomized and undercapitalized nature of the banks. Currently there are about 80 banks operating in Poland. Fifteen of them are quoted on the securities exchange.

The story of Petrobank SA gives a good idea of the way things are developing in banking in Poland. The account is given in Petrobank's

TABLE 12.1   Mergers and takeovers between the EU banks

Year	1985	1990	1992	1994	1996
Number	52	239	270	398	432

Source: Bandyk (1998).

Annual Report of 1997 supplemented by interviews with the Bank's executives.

THE COMPETITIVE STRENGTH OF THE PETROBANK SA

Petrobank SA is a relatively young bank on the Polish financial scene. It was instituted by decree of the President of the NBP (National Bank of Poland) in September 1990 under the name "Credit Company of Łódź – Bank SA" and its current name introduced at an Extraordinary General Meeting of shareholders on 4 March 1993. On 27 April 1995 it obtained the authorization of the Commission on Securities to put all its shares into public circulation and June 1995 saw a successful share issue. Quotations were given on the Warsaw Securities Exchange for the first time on 16 October 1995.

The dynamic development of Petrobank was noticed by the LG Group of Seoul, the third largest Korean capital group, where representatives put forward a proposal to increase the stock capital of the bank. As a result a letter of intent was signed on 28 December 1995, confirming that the LG Group had purchased 50% + 1 shares of Petrobank SA at the last issue. Subsequently (18 June 1996) Petrobank SA and the LG Securities Co Ltd concluded an Agreement of Partnership and an Agreement on Subscription of Shares.

Petrobank is a versatile bank, but it has based its activity on close cooperation with expanding and active Polish establishments which operate mainly in the fuel and energy area. It is also the main bank in its region. Figure 12.1 shows the distribution of its branches and offices.

Within six years of its inception the Petrobank had opened eight branches (in Łódź, Pabianice, Bydgoszcz, Kleszczów, Poznań, Warsaw, Olsztyn and Bełchatów), three agencies (two in Łódź and one in Bydgoszcz) and three pay-offices (two in Pabianice and one in Bełchatów). However, the board of directors felt increasingly that

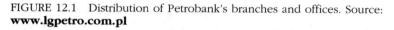

FIGURE 12.1   Distribution of Petrobank's branches and offices. Source:
www.lgpetro.com.pl

Petrobank was not in a position to compete effectively with foreign
banks or even with some of its Polish rivals. Apart from efficient
distribution, bank security, bank charges and commissions, the main
ingredient which contributes to success in the Polish market is the
existence of a wide choice of specialist services. Petrobank SA had
no new product with which to compete. Its Board of Directors of
Petrobank SA decided therefore to begin preparatory work on introducing a new product to the market: "home banking". Such a decision
seems all the more justified in light of the potential of using "home
banking" in itself to give a competitive edge.

- Results from research carried out in the USA show that the cost of
  banking operations settled by Internet is 100 times lower than
  traditional service.
- The development of this method of distributing bank products
  helps deal with the low level of traditional personal banking due
  to the low provision of banks per head of the Polish population
  compared with West European countries.
- Clearly developing "home banking" will be competitive in a
  situation where Polish banks as a whole are thinking of having to
  expand the number of their offices by at least a thousand (an
  increase of a third).

"Home banking" continues to be seen not only as a new bank product but as an instrument of distribution making it possible to cut costs.

"HOME BANKING" – CHARACTERISTICS OF THE PRODUCT

A special report in the *Businessman Magazine* in November 1995 gives details on "home banking". As one of those products using "electronic" banking, it has been in existence in developed banking systems for some time. "Home banking" makes it possible for the firm or individual utilizing it to have access to all the information related to their bank accounts without leaving their home or office. They can find out about current, credit, foreign currency and investment accounts, and look through extracts including detailed data related to the operations they have carried out. It is also possible for the bank to assemble accounts by their number or type and to look through some operations grouped according to determined criteria. The user can also effect intra- or interbank money movements, national and foreign transfers, and carry out periodic or permanent orders. The most important thing is that he or she can do it without any documents. This automatic system of making dispositions utilizes the auxiliary data-bases that include lists of contractors and current exchange rates or rates of interests of credits and deposits. In addition, it becomes much easier for the bank to monitor its own work.

For the banks themselves a most important aspect of "home banking" is that it reduces the need to build new branches. Further-more, such specialized computer systems do not require so many employees to be engaged in customer service. So there will be savings in both building investment and labour in the medium to long term.

There are many systems of electronic communication (Table 12.2). The most popular in Poland is Multi Cash, which is used by the ING, PeKaO SA and Creditanstalt. Some banks also use their own Polish systems. The CSBI – Corporate/Home Banking – installed its own system at almost all branches of its Credit Bank and at three branches of the Bank for Regional Cooperation.

Operating costs and the installation expenses of the system are fixed individually for each customer at most banks. At the Creditanstalt an installation fee charge of US$1200 per year is included in the annual fee.

TABLE 12.2 "Home banking" in Poland

	Name of system	Operating start	Number of customers	Operating costs and installation expenses
AmerBank	Electronic banking service Amer-Bank-Link	In course of installation	No data available	Unknown
Bank Gański	NetBank	1995	20	Individually negotiated
BIG	Home Banking	IV 1995	26	No data available
BPH	Home Banking	1995	ca 15 (testing)	Installation zl.1000; monthly fee from zl.300
BRE	Bresok	1993	650	Installation zl.300; monthly fee zl.70
Bank Śląski	Cash Management	XI 1995	3	Installation + modem zl.250; annuity zl.50
BWR	Home Banking	1995	3	Individually negotiated
CitiBank	Citibanking	EB – access to information from 1992; MTMS – start of payments from 1993	240	No data available
Creditanstalt	Multi Cash	XII 1995	185	$1200 a year
ING	Multi Cash	1994	ca 200	Installation free; monthly fee zl.300
PeKaO SA	Beta Multi Cash	VII 1995	ca 200	zl.1000 basic charge; zl.30 each following
PBI	Kontakt	VII 1995	ca 100	Min. monthly subscription zl.200
Pomorski Bank Kredytowy	Home Banking PBKS	1995	18	Installation zl.300; operating zl.200
Raiffaisen CentroBank	Electronic Banking	XI 1995	No data available	Individually negotiated
WBK	Minibank	VII 1994	20	Individually negotiated
Societe Generale	SGV Home Banking	I 1996 (new version)	No data available	No charges

Note: Roman numerals indicate the month of the year.

Source: *Rzeczpospolita*, 10 February 1996.

At the Polish Investment Bank the minimum monthly subscription is zl.200.

The main customers of "Home banking" are big firms well known to the bank and could be anything from a small number to several hundred. The Bank for Development of Export is the largest operator here with 650 firms on its books. PeKaO SA, ING and Creditanstalt already have about 200 customers each.

Questions

1. Indicate the possibilities and threats to the development of the Polish banking sector and evaluate the transformations in progress in it against a background of the banking market of the European Union.
2. Give potential sources of competitive superiority of Polish banks in the light of competition from foreign banks. Indicate the main marketing trends of foreign banks entering the Polish market.
3. Evaluate the possibilities of introducing "home banking" by the LG PetroBank. What possibilities for competitive superiority does this product give in the light of global competition?
4. Draw up and present together with the appropriate arguments a marketing plan for introducing a new product on to the market – "home banking".

References and further reading

Bandyk, K. (1998) World banking and findings for Poland. *Bank*. December.
Boruc, R. and Golata, K. (1996) Boom for credit; Wprost; August 1996. Annual Report – Petrobank.
Cary, T.P.A. (1989) Strategy formulation by bank. *International Journal of Bank Marketing*.
Central Bank. Publications of Central Bank.
Institute of Opinion and Market Research (1996) In-house.
Kowalik, F. (1998) Awake. *Newspaper of the Bank*. December.
Mazur, M. (1995) Jump of fortune. *Businessman Magazine*. November.
Wisniewska, M. (1998) Market for two or three. *Bank*. December.
www.lgpetro.com.pl (map of Petrobank branches).

13

Rocking the boat at MTV: dealing with market fragmentation

Ron Meyer and Ad Pruyn

Case	Strategic marketing
Main focus	Globalization, segmentation
Subsidiary focus	Advertising, branding
Scene	Europe, worldwide
Players	TV stations, young adults
Product	Television programmes

Summary

MTV is the leading music television broadcaster worldwide. The company is experiencing rapid growth and is highly profitable. Yet as the market for music television matures, fragmentation is also taking place. On the international scene, regional differences are surfacing and local competition is growing. Furthermore, in many markets, specialized niche broadcasters are targeting groups with different musical tastes. MTV is faced with the challenge of selecting its geographic and segment scope, and organizing itself in a way that it can deliver its broadcasting services to all of them. An additional complication is that MTV is in a fickle business, which requires that it keeps the loyalty of highly fashion-conscious young viewers. MTV must therefore remain youthful and retain its ability to constantly renew itself, despite being a huge billion-dollar corporation.

© 2000 John Wiley & Sons, Ltd.
Understanding Marketing: A European Casebook edited by Celia Phillips,
Ad Pruyn and Marie-Paule Kestemont.

Introduction

Here readers are presented with a problem which encourages some hard
thinking about the questions of optimal segmentation strategy. It is similar
to Case 9 on Coca-Cola in that American business is having to rethink its
general approach to this in the European context.

A company which has been highly segmented in terms of the age of its
target group, but has tried to aim at all countries under one brand, has to
face the fact that different countries or country groupings are now
producing a product which can threaten it in that territory. At the same
time their "safe" target audience is constantly changing its taste and ideas.
Keeping both these challenges in mind and remaining ahead of the game is
going to be very difficult for MTV.

An overview of MTV's development outside the USA is given since the
launch of MTV Networks Europe in 1987 as a "global" channel aimed at a
global youth culture. By 1996, pressure from national competitors who
were aiming at the same segment and advertisers who wanted to reach a
more national audience for their products pushed MTV towards more
localization in Europe and the setting up of five broadcasting areas.
Throughout the 1990s MTV has developed networks aimed at different
countries and country groupings – once again choosing to segment rather
than provide a worldwide service.

The latest challenges to MTV's supremacy are introduced – the constant
need to deal with pressure from video and record companies, the demand
to continue to attract good "world" brands, and problems of distribution.
Can MTV's strategies continue to work? This lively case gives ample basis
for discussion of this and other points connected with a new and
constantly changing product.

KEYWORDS

Globalization, localization, segmentation, branding, advertising,
Nielsen ratings, media.

Case

There are two things you need to know about MTV. The first, and this
is the good news, is that MTV just might be the best idea for a TV
network ever invented. That's because in its original and pure form,

MTV filled hour after hour of airtime with music videos supplied by record companies to promote their artists. What a concept! A network of commercials, interrupted only by more commercials and an occasional promotion (. . .) But the bad news is this: The channel must be constantly refreshed to stay current because pop music devours its young at a fearful pace (. . .).

To stay fresh, MTV is currently undergoing its most sweeping over-haul of the decade. The CEO intends to drive earnings by stretching and spinning the MTV and Nickelodeon brands into as many as a dozen new cable networks, feature films, online content, records, toys, clothes, books, and especially global markets. The results so far look promising, but there's always the danger that corporate pressures to exploit the brands could strain management, alienate consumers, or worst of all, leave those inside MTV Networks feeling as if they're no longer working in a hip, happening place but merely toiling for another money-hungry media giant like Fox, say, or Disney. Says Jeff Dunn, the chief operating officer of Nickelodeon: "How to maintain our guerrilla flavor when we've become the great corporate money-maker is a real challenge." Even Dunn, a preppy, Harvard-trained MBA, says that if the "suits" take over, MTV Networks is in trouble.

Marc Gunther, *Fortune*, 27 October 1997

Back in the 1980s, Mark Knopfler of Dire Straits sang "I want my MTV", and since then millions of people around the world have been granted this request. Launched in the USA in 1981, MTV was the first 24-hour music television network in the world, and has been the international leader ever since. It was the first network to have a presence on all five continents and currently reaches half of the television-owning households in the world. MTV is available to 298 million households in 82 countries around the globe, either via cable or by satellite.

MTV's first international move was the launch of MTV Networks Europe in 1987. During the first ten years, its philosophy was decidedly "global". Bill Roedy, head of MTV's international activities, strongly believed in an internationally standardized product and sought to create one network that would serve the entire continent from its base in London. In his view, the 18- to 24-year-olds that form the core of MTV's audience did not differ significantly from country to country, and would be attracted to the global youth culture projected by MTV. However, it did not take long for local competitors to emerge, such as Viva in Germany and Video Music in Italy, and these channels cut deeply into MTV's market share. Advertisers also complained that they did not need to reach a pan-European audience, but were more interested in national ones. Both pressures prompted Roedy to abandon his pan-European network in 1996 and to move towards more localization. His response has been to split the network into five services: MTV in the UK and Ireland, MTV Central (Austria, Germany and Switzerland), MTV Southern (Italy), MTV Nordic (Sweden, Finland, Norway and Denmark), and MTV Europe (35 countries including Spain, France, Belgium, the Netherlands, Greece, Israel and Eastern Europe). Within each of the five broadcasting areas MTV's "feed" can be split yet further, to allow for advertising focused on even smaller geographic territories. As of January 1999, MTV reaches approximately 62 million households across Europe, roughly the same number of households as it reaches in the USA.

After gaining experience in Europe, MTV started a Portuguese-language MTV Brasil in 1990. The next step was to expand to the rest of the continent by launching MTV Networks Latin America in 1993. This Spanish-language network offers two separate services. The northern feed, coming from Mexico City, is directed towards Bolivia, Colombia, Ecuador, Venezuela, Central America, the Caribbean, Mexico and parts of the USA. The southern feed, originating from Buenos Aires, is distributed to Argentina, Chile, Paraguay, Peru and Uruguay. In all, 25 million households across Latin America have access to MTV.

The next step was to launch MTV Networks Asia with its head-quarters in Singapore in 1995. Its first service was the Chinese-language MTV Mandarin, which is transmitted via satellite to China, Taiwan, Brunei, Singapore and South Korea. The English-language MTV Southeast Asia was started almost simultaneously to serve the Philippines, Malaysia, Brunei, Hong Kong, Indonesia, Papua New Guinea, Singapore, South Korea, Thailand and Vietnam. In 1996 the English-language MTV India was added, reaching India, Bangladesh, Nepal, Sri Lanka, Pakistan and the Middle East. Together, over 100 million households across Asia can tune in to MTV.

Most recent moves have been the launch of MTV Australia in 1997 and MTV Russia in 1998. The latter is particularly remarkable, as MTV is the first Western television network to create a customized service for the Russian market. The Russian-language programming is made in Moscow and is broadcast "free-as-air" in most of the country's large cities.

A large part of MTV's success is attributable to the network's ability to understand, follow and even shape the volatile audience of teens and twenty-somethings in a way that suit-and-tie-wearing executives at stuffier networks have found difficult to imitate. MTV has consistently been able to strike a chord with the fickle group of young adults, who appreciate its unpredictable and irreverent approach. By being at the forefront of new trends, MTV has become essential for those who want to know what is fashionable. This has made MTV more than a TV channel – it is a part of the youth culture. While focused on the group of 18- to 24-year-olds, MTV picks up many viewers in the 12- to 17-year-old segment, who can't wait to be 18, and among the 25- to 34-year-old group, who want to stay young as long as possible. In most countries, few other networks have catered to these specific segments, and this has opened the door for MTV's entrance into the market.

However, in broadcasting, good channel format and a receptive target audience are not enough to guarantee success. It also depends on a network's ability to manage relationships with a number of key external stakeholders:

- *First, a channel needs suppliers – someone must provide MTV with videos.* At this moment, the record companies produce these highly expensive videos as promotional devices to sell their CDs and supply them free of cost to music channels. But while both sides benefit from this relationship, it places the record companies in a relatively dependent position. If MTV decides not to broadcast a new video, record companies have few alternatives. Unsurprisingly, the record companies would be happy if MTV had more competitors. It is not a good omen for MTV that its leading challenger in Germany, VIVA, was initiated by the record companies PolyGram, EMI Music, Sony and Time Warner.
- *Secondly, advertisers are essential to the survival of a TV channel.* Most commercial broadcasters do not rely on viewers to pay for the programmes watched (either by subscription or pay as you

view), but largely finance operations out of advertising revenues. This is also true for MTV, which is heavily dependent on attracting enough advertisers interested in its youth segment. Some advertisers have become whole-hearted partners of MTV. For instance, PepsiCo has a long-term relationship with MTV, with the intention of co-promoting both brands and reinforcing each other's positions worldwide. However, there are not very many companies that want the international advertising that MTV is so good at offering outside of the USA. Furthermore, many advertisers in the USA would not mind some competition for MTV, to keep advertising prices down.

- *A third success factor for TV channels is distribution.* Programmes need to reach viewers' TV sets, either by satellite, cable or through the airwaves. Transmitting via satellite is relatively simple. Satellite "slots" can be rented from third parties and viewers can receive transmissions with a dish. However, in most countries the number of households with a dish is quite low, given the high initial cost, ranging from 1000 to 3000 Euros. Because of this most commercial channels prefer distribution via cable systems, which have a high level of penetration in most developed economies. Yet getting cable operators to carry a channel often proves to be an arduous task. Most cable operators have small regional monopolies and need to be convinced of the need to make extra costs to carry an additional channel. Many cable systems are technically limited to a fixed number of channels and therefore they need to drop an existing broadcaster before a new channel can be accommodated. This gives cable companies quite a bit of power, leading operators in some countries to demand that commercial channels pay for a slot on the cable.

Although MTV has been at the top of the charts for more than 15 years, other channels have been steadily rising in the ratings and challenge MTV's virtual ownership of the youth market. In the USA, real competition has only recently emerged. The Canadian network MuchMusic launched a channel in the USA in 1994 and by 1997 was also present in Mexico, Argentina and Finland. The Box, a channel that allows viewers to call in and select the videos to be played, has been doing moderately well, expanding from the USA to the UK, the Netherlands, Argentina, Peru and Chile. MOR Music Television is a music-shopping network that combines videos with merchandising breaks. Besides these general music channels, MTV is facing a number of competitors focusing on only one type of music. BET on Jazz, Black Entertainment Television, The Nashville Network, Country Music Television, The Gospel Network and Z Music (Christian) may all draw viewers away from MTV.

Outside its home base, competition varies by country, but is becoming fierce in a number of mature markets. For instance, in Germany MTV has lost its top spot to VIVA, which employs German-speaking DJs and mixes international and local music. The same is true in the Netherlands, where a local player, The Music Factory, is knocking MTV off front stage. In the UK, The Box pulled ahead of MTV in 1997 and a new entrant, UK Play, has launched an assault. In all these cases the competitive advantage of MTV's new rivals is their ability to tailor programming to the demands of the local market.

Taken together, these developments form a rather tricky strategic problem for MTV. As the market for music television is maturing, it seems to be fragmenting. The market seems to be disintegrating into niches along musical and geographic lines. Competitors are focusing on one type of music or one country, outspecializing the generalist MTV.

So far, MTV's response has been to follow the trend towards narrower target audiences and more specific programming content. Internationally, MTV seems to be moving further and further away from its strategy of international standardization, towards localized programming with an international flavour. As for segmentation along musical lines, MTV is endeavouring to offer a broad range of different formats to cover different musical tastes. MTV's oldest spinoff is VH-1, which is also a 24 hours a day music channel, directed towards an audience of 25- to 40-year-olds, who want a mix of "classics" and easily digestible contemporary music. VH-1 is doing well in the USA and has been moving abroad in the last few years. It is now more popular than MTV in the UK. Another move has been the launch of M2 in the US market in August 1996. M2 is an all-video channel that closely resembles the early free-form MTV, before it began running more long-form non-music programmes. Industry analysts remark that even if M2 does not break even, it might block the way for new competitors and should satisfy record companies' complaints that MTV does not offer enough airtime to new acts.

MTV's latest move has been to spawn a new range of MTV brand extensions. MTV Extra has been created with the intention of focusing on playing independent rock. MTV Base is a channel playing soul and rap, and VH-1 Classics plays pop and rock from the late 1970s and early 1980s. One of the critical factors that will determine these channels' success is whether advertisers are willing to buy airtime. Nielsen ratings are usually important for determining advertising spending, but these ratings are notoriously unable to track the viewing and channel surfing behaviour of the young music audience, rendering them quite unreliable. Advertisers must therefore be willing to place "trust" in MTV's ability to reach, and connect with, the intended target audience.

In the medium to long term, the most important factor in determining whether MTV remains successful might be its ability to constantly renew itself and remain youthful. It is hard work staying at the cutting edge of pop culture. It requires constant undermining of everything that has become established. MTV has now become part of the music establishment – but it cannot permit itself to act as such. It must ride the next wave of youth culture. The struggle continues. At the moment the average age of MTV employees is 28 years and there are more people with nose rings than neckties. The only corporate dress code, jokes CEO Tom Freston, is "no full-frontal nudity". Nevertheless, as the company grows and new channels are added, the threat of becoming a regular corporation increases. Add to this the pressure from MTV's owner, the media giant Viacom, to exploit the MTV brand through films, records, toys, clothes, books and other merchandising, and the threat of becoming an ordinary company becomes apparent. Or as the employee quoted at the beginning of this case put it: "How to maintain our guerrilla flavor when we've become the great corporate moneymaker is a real challenge."

Whether MTV's moves towards localization and brand extensions will prove to be the best possible response to the fragmentation of the music television market remains to be seen. And whether MTV's company culture can retain its youthful rebelliousness and creativity as the company grows is also an issue on the minds of the company's top management. In short, MTV has some difficult nuts to crack – which is not exactly what Mark Knopfler meant when he sang about getting "your money for nothing and your chicks for free".

Questions

1. What are the advantages gained by MTV by being a global player?
2. How strong are the pressures for further localization of MTV's services?
3. How can MTV balance the demands of global operations and local responsiveness?
4. Which "musical segments" do you recognize in your national market?
5. In which segments is MTV vulnerable to new specialist music channels?
6. How can MTV convince advertisers of their reach, given the unreliability of the Nielsen ratings?
7. How should MTV respond to possible fragmentation and specialist competition?
8. How should MTV respond to new media, in particular to broadcasting via the Internet?
9. How should MTV be organized to operate in all of these countries, segments and media, while remaining young, rebellious and innovative?

Acknowledgements

This case is based on work published in De Wit and Meyer (see References and further reading).

References and further reading

Baird, R. (1999) MTV chief faces euro challenge. *Marketing Week* April 22.
Burgi, M. (1997) MTV turns up the music. *Mediaweek* November 17.

De Wit, B. and Meyer, R. (1998) *Strategy – Process, Content and Context: An International Perspective*. London: International Thomson Publishing.

Fry, A. (1998) The European perspective. *Marketing* October 1.

Gunther, M. (1997) This gang controls your kids' brains. *Fortune* October 27.

Gunther, M. (1999) Viacom: Redstone's remarkable ride to the top. *Fortune* April 26.

Higgins, J.M. (1997) McGrath shakes up MTV. *Broadcasting & Cable* November 17.

Higgins, J.M. (1999) Invasion of the Viacom people. *Broadcasting & Cable* April 12.

Hudes, K. (1997) Windows on the world. *Mediaweek* December 1.

Marchand, N. (1999) NCTC and MTV settle. *Broadcasting & Cable* April 5.

The Economist (1998) Business: Star woes. April 11.

14

Czech beer goes worldwide

Jana Nagyova and Hana Machkova

Case	Market entry strategy
Main focus	Market segmentation, consumer habits
Subsidiary focus	Trade barriers, licensing, partnership
Scene	The Czech Republic, Europe, worldwide
Players	Beer industry, competitors, consumers
Product	Beer

Summary

The Czech Republic has always had a strong "beer" culture. It is the home of Pilsner style beer and its inhabitants have the highest consumption of beer per head in the world.

A fall in local consumption of beer and resulting over-capacity of Czech breweries has led them to look to an international market.

What marketing strategies should Czech beer producers and exporters adopt in order to develop existing brands or begin new ones in foreign markets?

Introduction

Like Case 2, this case looks at possible strategies in the beer industry. Given the three further cases in the cold drinks sectors (8, 9, and 15), it is clear that contributors find this an interesting area!

Readers do not have far to look for a reason in this example. The production of beer is booming in the Czech Republic and, while its home market has always been loyal and contained high consumers of Czech beer products, its new neighbour (once classed as a home consumer) Slovakia is raising tariffs to protect its own beer industry. Assuming that consumers in the Czech Republic will not buy any more beer (the solution favoured by Hungarian Case 2 or Coca-Cola in Germany in Case 9), a strong exporting strategy will be needed.

The case provides us with the background facts and figures we need to be able to discuss this: the main beer-consuming countries are given, and the three leading Czech breweries introduced. Figures both of imported beer as a proportion of beer consumption in the main consuming countries and actual exports to these countries in terms of the Czech beer industry are given. This case gives readers the opportunity to think about the problems associated with market entry in an international context not merely from a conceptual viewpoint but with a reasonable collection of figures to use for evidence.

KEYWORDS

Entry strategies, export, licensing, trade barriers, Czech beer, international beer consumer habits.

Case

Example of the most successful brand of Czech beer (from the daily *Hospodarske noviny*, 24 September 1997):

Budvar has nearly doubled its production in the last few years

The Budějovice brewery received the Giovanni Marcora international prize from the European Union

Česke Budějovice (Budweiser) – In four years Budweiser Budvar nearly doubled its production from 590 000 hl in 1992 to 1.026 million hl last year (1996). Exports of beer in this period grew from 362 000 to 495 000 hl. In the first half of this year, the brewery produced 531 710 hl of beer, which is 6.2% more than the same period in 1996. Its export represents a growth of 12.9%. In total, this year Budvar will sell abroad about 600 000 hl of beer from an anticipated production of 1.150 million hl. In six months of this year sales rose by CZK936 million (about 17 million Euros), which is 17.8% more than in the same period last year. The profit enhanced about CZK240 million.

Economic manager of the Česke Budějovice brewery Petr Jansky considers the growth of exports a permanent feature, in spite of the fact that the European beer market is oversaturated. At the beginning of the 1990s, the company exported to 18 countries, but now the figure is 48 countries. Jansky predicts that by the end of the year (1997), the number of countries will reach 50. For example, the company exported 220 000 hl of beer to Germany last year. Among foreign brands, Budvar came in at third place directly behind the Danish brands Tuborg and Fax. Tuborg (460 000 hl), however, has most of its so-called exports executed by its own brewery in Monchengladbach. According to Jansky, it is necessary to exercise patience, because results will not be apparent immediately. "In Britain, we are selling 100 000 hectalitres (hl) this year, whereas years ago we began with only a few thousand hl. A similar situation is taking place now in Russia. Last year we sold less than 4000 hl. This year we are selling more than 25 000 hl, and we predict that in following period it will be 100 000 hl of beer," he said.

Jansky added that Budvar received the Giovanni Marcora prize for the year 1996, awarded by the agricultural commission of the European Union, for being the most progressive company in foodstuffs, agriculture and ecology. "In the context of prizes which we have received in the past few years, this affair departs from the norm. The company did not get the prize – as it received prizes in previous years – for the quality of its product, but rather for the overall level of operations and dynamic progress," said Jansky. He also called attention to the fact that only current member states of the European Union had received such an award up till then.

The production of beer has a long and illustrious history in the Czech Republic. The first brew of the "Pilsner type", the beer which later became popular with beer drinkers worldwide as the PILS beer and which owes its name to the town of Pilsner (Plzen), was produced in that town in 1842. Since then, Czech beer of the Pilsner variety has developed a world class reputation for superior quality. Another well-known brand was born in the country. In 1895 a joint-stock brewery – today's Budweiser Budvar – was founded in the town of Budweis (Česke Budějovice). That company nowadays uses the internationally protected trade marks Budweiser beer and Budweiser Budvar.

Although all the ingredients for Czech world class beer production remain (intense competition, world class products and suppliers, and discriminating home demand), the lustre of the beer industry was tarnished by the legacy of communist rule and central planning. Central planning meant that the beer sector, in common with others, was plagued by under-investment and the uneconomic allocation of resources. Pilsner Urquell and Budvar were in fact the only products for which the central planners provided export support. Further, at the end of the 1980s, the market for Czech beer in Central and Eastern Europe (CEE) collapsed under the strain of tariffs and other protective trade barriers.

However, the Czech beer sector is in the middle of a dramatic transition and renaissance. Beer producers have made significant investments in new production equipment and technology. Marketing and distribution investments are on the rise and are increasingly important as customer needs and distribution channels change. Beer producers compete with each other for domestic market share. Competitive pressure will intensify. During this industry turmoil, some beer producers have been attaining positions of export leadership while others are forced to leave the market.

Profitability throughout the sector has been negatively affected by a shift away from premium beer, stagnation in domestic sales, artificially low prices and low levels of exports. Fierce competition, low operating margins, and trade barriers have compelled breweries to reduce costs and build a low-cost production base. Ironically, the difficult competitive environment has made Czech beer producers internationally price-competitive. In addition, low industry profitability since privatization has forced breweries to restructure. Continued industry restructuring and consolidation are anticipated. It will become increasingly harder for small and medium breweries to remain in business and it is anticipated that consolidation will accelerate to finish around the millennium.

In 1996, production of beer in the Czech Republic was 18.24 million hl. Total domestic consumption was more than 16.5 million hl and exports stood at 1.8 million hl. The six largest companies produced more than 12.7 million hl of beer, accounting for 69.8% of total domestic capacity. Products from the largest breweries took 67.4% of domestic consumption. Their share of Czech exports was 92%.

The Czech Republic still has the world's highest per capita consumption of beer (160 litres per year). Table 14.1 compares consumption in several countries. The data show that, although countries such as Denmark and Germany also have high per capita beer consumption, they cannot rival the Czech Republic! Some countries such as China and Italy have extremely low consumption by any standards.

TABLE 14.1 Average annual per capita beer consumption in selected countries, 1998

	(litres)
Czech Republic	160
Germany	137
Denmark	125
UK	101
Italy	25
China	12

Source: Bass 1998, reproduced with their permission.

It is predicted that overall domestic consumption will stagnate and/or gradually decline following changes in lifestyle in the coming years. In addition, potential consumers with improving purchasing power may shift from standard to premium beers and the shift to this heavier and more expensive version will not necessarily lead to higher consumption levels. Lower class, low-income consumers will most likely continue to prefer cheap beers, as they will remain highly price-sensitive. Czechs drink most beer at weekends, but overall beer consumption is still relatively high on workdays. Approximately 50% of adults (over 18 years) drink more than one beer (0.5 litres) a day.

Three big breweries have export potential, Budweiser Budvar, Pilsner Urquell and Prague Breweries, the last of which has a strong foreign investor (it has had a joint venture with UK Bass since 1994). The export figures for Czech beers grow every year. Budweiser Budvar is the largest exporter. It increased its exports for the first six months of 1997 by 13% over the same period in 1996. Pilsner Urquell also registered an increase in exports, and its goal is to regularly increase its yearly exports by roughly a fifth. Finally, Prague Breweries are the fastest growing exporter in the Czech Republic, with growth of 23% per annum, owing in particular to its support from Bass (Table 14.2).

TABLE 14.2   Export volumes by groups in 1997

	Hectolitres
Budweiser Budvar	540 262
Pilsner Urquell	457 871
Prague Breweries	419 239

Source: Prague Breweries 1998.

Looking at Czech beers in foreign markets, we can also see expansion. In the German market, for example, according to data compiled by the Union of German Breweries, the most successful foreign brand was Tuborg (Denmark) with 460 000 hl, followed by Fax (Denmark) and Budvar, both with 220 000 hl. Pilsner Urquell and Staropramen (a brand from Prague Breweries) both had 60 000 hl and tied in eighth place. Total imports of beer into Germany in 1996 were 3.5 million hl, which comprised a mere 3% of total consumption. Consumption of foreign beer, however, increased in 1996 against the previous year by 7%, and according to exporters it could attain up to 10% of total consumption. Nevertheless there is a common problem for all exporters: the strong brand loyalty of local consumers in beer segments, which is demonstrated in Table 14.3.

Table 14.3 shows the small proportion of beer imported in the large traditional markets. One way of dealing with this is to enter new markets and Czech breweries consider Russia a (good) prospective market. It is one of the biggest consumers of hard alcohol in the world – but perhaps they can be persuaded to drink beer. Consumers still

TABLE 14.3   Imported beers as a percentage of total
local consumption in selected countries

	1996	1998*	2000*
Belgium	5.6	5.9	6.0
Czech Republic	0.4	0.4	0.4
Hungary	1.9	1.8	2.4
Germany	2.8	3.5	4.2
Poland	0.5	0.4	0.9
Austria	4.8	5.2	5.6
Slovakia	13.2	9.6	9.3

* Estimate.

Source: Canadead Limited in *Hospodarske Noviny* 17.2.1998.

prefer vodka but it is probable that little by little new consumption habits will assert themselves, and there is evidence of a slight switch to light alcohol drinks. This could mean a great opportunity for Czech beers.

Czech beer prices when compared internationally are extremely low. Those low prices are artificial – another legacy of the planned system. Up to now price increases implemented by brewers have been below inflation (currently around 10% per year). This is changing, however: in 1998, an annual price hike of up to 3% or more over inflation was expected.

Since the Velvet Revolution, the Czech brewing sector has generally underperformed with respect to exports. However, we have seen a strong recovery in sales to the traditional CEE markets. Experts give a conservative forecast of an average annual export growth rate of at least 10% through the year 2000, when exports should reach 3–6 million hectolitres. Figure 14.1 shows export destinations for Czech beer in 1996.

The use of exporting as an entry strategy for beer can be complicated by trade barriers (tariffs, taxes on consumption, quotas, etc.). The Slovak government has, for example, introduced quotas for imports of Czech beers in order to protect their local producers. This means Czech breweries will need to use techniques other than traditional sales methods in order to emerge in foreign markets. An article from the daily *MF Dues* (12 September 1997) shows they intend to do this.

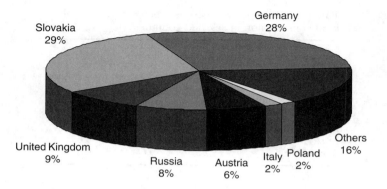

FIGURE 14.1   Where did Czech breweries export in 1996? Source: Výzkumý ústav pivovarský a sladařský, 1997.

BREWERIES WANT TO EXPAND PRODUCTION ABROAD

Thanks to their extraordinary success in the past few years, the strongest domestic breweries will begin to produce their own brands directly in foreign countries. This route is led by Pilsner Urquell, though even Budweiser Budvar is thinking about moving its breweries abroad. (Budvar was the largest exporter in 1997.) Breweries at least partly want to move away from the trade barriers that restrict imports of beer to, for example, Slovakia or Russia.

"Originally, we were proud that Budvar would produce only in (the city of) České Budějovice (Budweiser). Now, however, we are thinking about selling the brewing license abroad," said Robert Chart, sales director of the Budweiser Company.

Pilsner Urquell already has experience with producing beer abroad. In July 1997 it began licensing the production of its Gambrinus brand in the Lithuanian brewery Ragutis. The company is preparing a similar project in Saransko (Russia) and in Zlatý Bažant (Slovakia). Pilsner Urquell even looks to the South American markets.

The Pilsner brewery, which exports approximately one-tenth of production, believes in a further reinforcement of its positions abroad through a connection with the second domestic brewery Radegast. Nomura, which is trying to enter these two companies, intends export expansion for both into the eastern market.

Prague Breweries will also make use of a connection with a foreign partner. The British brewery concern Bass, which is its majority shareholder, is establishing the beers Staropramen and Vratislavice on the British Isles. For example, Vratislavice 12°, under the name Czech Lager, is currently available in all Tesco supermarkets. Staropramen entered the British market in 1993 thanks to Bass, and since that time sales have grown continuously. Last year, for example, roughly 40 000 hl of Smíchov beer was sold in the UK.

"In the first six months of this year, the sales of Staropramen in Great Britain grew 23% against the same period last year," said Prague Breweries spokeswoman Diana Dobálová (*MF Dues*, September 1997).

Questions

1. What are the main arguments of Czech brewers for foreign market entry?
2. Analyse the market environment for breweries in your country; describe existing competitor positions. Draw a perceptual map.
3. Find an ideal position for a Czech brand, define the proper marketing strategy, and outline the marketing plan to reach that position.
4. Define the key success factors for the new entrant, and recommend the mode of entry for Czech breweries.

References and further reading

Czech Mate (1997) Bass and OPB face off in fermenting conflict. *The Wall Street Journal Europe*. January 24–25.
Lees G. (1996) *Good Beer Guide to Prague and the Czech Republic*. London: CAMRA Books.
Smith, D.E. and Heede, S. (1996) The north–south divide: changing patterns in the consumption of alcoholic beverages in Europe. *Proceedings, 25th EMAC Conference*, Vol. 1, Budapest University of Economic Sciences.

15

Alcopops: triumph or disaster?

Celia Phillips

Case	New product
Main focus	Market segmentation, market saturation
Subisidary focus	Youth consumption, ethics, fashion market
Scene	UK
Players	Government, regulatory mechanisms, consumers
Product	Alcoholic lemonade

Summary

This case looks at the problems experienced by producers and retailers when they aim to target a product at a particular age group (children) with its associated ethical considerations. The "history" of alcopops in the UK – their arrival from Australia and brief boom in 1996 and 1997 followed by rapid contraction – is given. The implications of this kind of specialization for companies endeavouring to increase their overall sales are discussed and the general problem of declining alcohol sales in Europe as a whole.

Introduction

Case 15 looks at the introduction of a new product – the alcopop. Alcoholic lemonade and its relations – the "coolers" and "spritzers" – are fairly well known in most countries and the background to their development – the saturation of the beer and wine markets in many countries – commonplace. What has been different about the marketing of alcopops is the opportunistic way in which a new product was aimed at a particular market and the rapidity of the rise and fall of the consequent craze. Ethical considerations and the question of possible government regulation over the advertising and sales of such products are also of interest.

Students from different countries will be surprised by certain aspects of this case. In many places (in particular the USA) the idea that people under 18 or even 21 could easily obtain products with a slightly higher alcohol content than beer is astonishing and clearly immoral. However, in Britain, in the late 1990s such a thing was possible and appears to have formed the base of a briefly, lucrative new product. It seems as if this phenomenon was not observed in other European countries apart from Ireland and Switzerland with its "Moo-milk alcopop". One of the advantages of this case is that readers can revisit the idea of a new product and clearly relate it to problems with segmentation.

As with many new product stories, the initial development of alcopops followed from a new supply of raw materials and a good idea. An Australian lemon harvest and an entrepreneurial local brewer led to a "fun" local product. Within two years the new product had arrived in the UK The case follows the proliferation of sub-products and flavours, brands and advertising campaigns and public concern about the implicit market of under-age drinkers. Though obstensibly aimed at women non-drinkers and young adults, media reports make it clear that alcopops swiftly became an "in drink" for the under 18s and were sometimes bought by under 16s.

An interesting feature of the case lies in the fact that sales had begun to decline before products were withdrawn from retail and restaurant outlets and the names of the products had been changed to deter the young. Was the craze over? Did distributors react to their own falling profits rather than government and media reaction? What are the implications for future products which may become popular with the lower end of the youth market? These questions all fit in to a case which helps readers investigate the development of new differentiated products in a crowded market.

KEYWORDS

Alcopops, alcoholic carbonates, alcoholic soft drinks, alcoholic lemonades, youth consumption, consumer segmentation, targeting, ethics.

Case

THE STORY 1993–1998

The Australian summer of 1993 (November/December) was good for lemons – and Duncan MacGillivray brewed up a neighbour's crop. Called Two Dogs alcoholic lemonade, it was "on tap" in 100 local pubs within six months. By September 1994 it was bottled for wider sale. "Alcopops" (alias alcoholic carbonates or alcoholic lemonade) were born.

So far, development of the product had been opportunistic – a result of the combination of a glut of lemons, a good summer, and the acceptance of a "fun" product. The next stage – export to the UK by Inchcape Marketing Distributor – was premeditated (Zenith, November 1994). The market for alcoholic drink in the UK, and Europe generally, was flagging. The Euromonitor figures for the period (Euromonitor, September 1995) give a general picture of a saturated beer market for most countries, hope for a slight rise in demand for wine in the UK and Belgium, and a large rise in non-alcoholic drinks in France. Perhaps the rapid success of "Two Dogs" could be repeated in such markets.

The product (alcoholic lemonade with 4.5–5.5% alcohol – comparable to, and sometimes stronger than, lager) was an instant success in the UK. According to Mintel reports, sales by value were:

1995   £90 million
1996   £265 million (with an estimate for 2000 of £335 million)

Though the 1996 figures only compared with 1% of beer sales, competitors had sprung up from other companies and sales had been taken from the premium cider, premium lager, and spirit mixer markets. Two Dogs (now distributed by Merrydown) and Hoopers

Hooch (Bass) dominated the market, but all major brewers launched at least one rival product and Sainsbury's supermarket also developed an own brand. The Mintel account of 1996 (Mintel, March 1997) is an exciting marketing read: "The alcoholic soft drinks market has seen rapid rates of growth since the launch of the first brands in Summer 1995, with a rush of new products aimed at capitalising on the buoyant success of the market". Success on an international level made this "the fastest growing new alcohol product of all time".

At this point the market had the following products:

- Hoopers Hooch (Bass) in four flavours, which made up two-thirds of sales by value
- Shott's Alcoholic Selzer (launched March 1996)
- Two Dogs (Merrydown), which made up 5% of sales by value

Other major players were Woody's (Beverage Brands), Punchers (Thornlodge) and Jammin (Spilt Drinks), but there were over 30 brands at this point.

Writers of the Mintel report felt that only four or five brands would stay the distance. They would be characterized by having

- Invested in marketing and production
- Developed an individual identity/niche market

Advertising spent in the year up to December 1996 was £2.7 million on 25 brands. Hoopers Hooch had £865 000 spent on it, and other major spenders were

- Schott's Alcoholic Selzer Sub Zero
- Taunton's Diamond "Zest"
- and Carlsberg–Tetley's Lemonhead exotic

Some new brands that year were

- Fizi (made of kava kava)
- Wild Brew (made of guarava – an exotic fruit)

Even the generally rather staid Sainsbury's produced a lemon alcopop called "Piranha". Their strategic marketing director Anthony Rees said "We feel the name "Piranha" has got a bit more bite to it than plain Sainsbury's alcoholic lemonade."

By mid 1997, alcopops made up 5% of the UK alcoholic drinks market and, according to the chairman of Merrydown, the market had been flooded by 90 new brands since summer 1995. By October 1997, the estimate of sales for the whole year was £400 million.

In the event, the 1997 figure was £300 million and suddenly the estimates reverse – 1997 estimates for the value of alcopop sales (Mintel, March 1997) were

1998	£190 million
1999	£160 million
2000	£148 million
2001	£140 million
2002	£135 million

What had happened? Was this a case of a sudden craze and two good summers, or an over-expanded market – or had other factors come into play?

THE TARGET CUSTOMERS

From the outset, Two Dogs distributors and other manufacturers maintained that their target was women non-drinkers and young adults, and the Euromonitor figures for May 1996 go some way to supporting this. The typical drinker was aged 18–31 and a higher than average proportion were women (40 to 50%).

Later that year Mintel commissioned BMRB to undertake a survey of the levels of usage of alcopops and consumer attitudes towards them. 1433 over-18-year-olds were interviewed. However, in view of the strong feeling that consumers younger than 18 were trying alcopops, a student project used the same question on 232 London 13–18-year-olds (Hamon 1997).

Table 15.1 shows Haman's results for under 18s as to their knowledge of the product and whether they have tried it. Clearly, a

TABLE 15.1 Knowledge and use of alcopops (1997)

| | Age group (inclusive) percentage | |
	13–15	16–18
Know the product	64	78
Found it attractive	57	72
Have tried it	18	42
Of those who tried:		
Regular	5 ⎱ 11	48 ⎱ 60
Occasional	6 ⎰	12 ⎰
Buy it	4	10

Source: Hamon (1997). Reproduced with permission.

large number of the 16–18 age group had tried alcopops, and a solid proportion of them were regular drinkers.

Nearly two-thirds of 13–15-year-olds knew of the products and more than a half found them attractive. Nearly one-fifth had tried them. The overall figure for *women* to have tried them is 41% in the BMRB survey. For all 18–24-year-olds it is 82%. Forty-five per cent of 18–24-year-olds said they drank regularly or occasionally. Clearly, the market reach for alcopops fell well below the age of 18 – and women were not perhaps the most significant market.

A few figures from the two surveys add further detail. Negative and positive ideas of the product were tested. Results are shown in Table 15.2. Some older people saw alcopops as a refreshing alternative to cider or beer, while a third of those in the younger groups saw them as "trendy" and "for young people" – a clear niche market to them!

On the whole the older group had more negative feelings about alcopops (Table 15.3). Clearly quite a high proportion of adults interviewed felt that alcopops encouraged under-age drinking. (Only about a third of under 18-year-olds agreed – perhaps they felt they didn't need encouragement!) More of the adults than the under 18s felt that they couldn't see the point of the product and that it was not clearly labelled as alcohol. The 13–15-year-olds were the most sceptical – over a third said alcopops were a craze!

When asked the single best and worst thing about the product, the 13–15s gave taste (54%) as the best and the fact that it was alcohol (69%) as the worst. The 16–18s gave "trendy" (45%) as the best and "price" (54%) as the worst.

TABLE 15.2   Positive ideas about alcopops, by age group, percentages (1996[†], 1997[*])

Ideas about product	Age group		
	13–15[*]	16–18[*]	over 18[†]
Trendy	35	34	28
For young people	35	37	23
Refreshing alternative to cider or beer	8	9	17
Summer drink	17	15	16

Source: Mintel (1997)[†] and Hamon (1997)[*]. Reproduced with permission.

TABLE 15.3   Negative ideas about alcopops, by age group, percentages (1996[†], 1997[*])

	Age group		
	13–15[*]	16–18[*]	over 18[†]
Encourages under-age drinking	32	36	59
Can't see point of product	17	15	32
Not clearly labelled as alcohol	21	15	27
Craze – won't last	38	28	21

Source: Mintel (1997)[†] and Hamon (1997)[*]. Reproduced with permission.

Based on these figures, which were nationwide for BMRB but London-based for Hamon, it is fairly clear that, while one could argue that women and young adults were possible niche markets, under 18s were another, and the 16–18 group were probably more likely to drink alcopops than 18–24-year-olds.

What bearing does this have on our story?

THE MEDIA, POLITICIANS, AND PRESSURE GROUPS

From the outset, worries had been expressed about the likely consumers of alcopops. The 1996 Euromonitor report notes that off trade sales (such as supermarkets where there can be little control of the consumer) were increasing (they eventually made up more than half of product sales) and that alcohol awareness groups were worried that the sweetness of the drinks masked alcohol and could encourage under-age drinking, as also could the use of the word "lemonade", traditionally associated with children's drinks.

By January 1996, *The Times* newspaper reported that the Portman Group (an industry-funded body which aims to promote responsible drinking) was working overtime to lay down rules about the naming, packaging and point-of-sale promotion of alcopops. TNT Liquid Dynamite's bright red packaging in the shape of a stick of dynamite was said to be "unacceptable" for using dangerous imagery – and withdrawn. In August a report in the *British Medical Journal* gave figures on drunkenness for 750 school children in Dundee (Scotland). Incidence of reported drunkenness was higher in children who had tried the more exotic alcopops. In May 1997, *The Birmingham Post* reported that hospitals in the Midlands had seen increases in admissions for children suffering from alcohol poisoning. Bass, the manufacturer of Hoopers Hooch, was also officially rebuked by Portman's for using cartoons to promote their alcoholic lemonade. The brewery henceforth cleared all its advertisements with Portman's. In the same month a 14-year-old boy burned down his school while allegedly drunk on alcoholic lemonade. The Home Secretary ordered a government inquiry into alcocops. July saw reports of undercover teenage "alcopops" who were to help detect shopkeepers selling alcohol to underage drinkers. Police were given powers to confiscate alcohol from under 18s drinking in public.

How did manufacturers and retailers respond? By August 1997, Bass was considering a relaunch of Hoopers Hooch and blackcurrant flavoured Hooch was withdrawn. It was too popular with the young (the report in *The Independent* stated that more than three million cans and bottles of Hooch were sold every week). Scottish Courage (distributors for Merrydown) announced that it was revamping Two Dogs in order to appeal to "women" and "older customers".

In May 1997, the Spar supermarket (2200 stores in Britain) dropped its own brand alcopops. In August Sainsbury's axed its own label (Piranha had been renamed "alcoholic lemon drink" in December 1996), while the Coop, Safeways and Iceland ceased sales of *all* alcopops. In addition, Weatherspoons, a chain of 194 public houses, banned alcopops from *all* their outlets. Whitbreads, a larger chain, banned them from the 400 family pubs of their 1700 total. Portman's also criticized several other brands in May – either for their names, or their packaging – and five, including Barking Frog (AlliedDomecq) and WKD Red, were withdrawn. Moo – an alcoholic milk drink – was renamed to make it less appealing to under 18s.

All this should have indeed led to a fall in consumption, if only because of the fall in brands and outlets for buying alcopops, but it is interesting to note that the drop in purchases came before this disastrous August.

THE DECLINE IN PURCHASING OF ALCOPOPS

Harpers reported the first month on month fall in sales between April and May 1997. Total sales fell by 30% over that month, and sales from supermarkets and off-licences by 42%. *Marketing Week*, in its report "The Bubble Bursts" (September 1997), gave its most recent bimonthly figures which showed that sales in May/June 1997 were 14% down on the same months for 1996. They blamed these changes on "cooler weather" and competition from pre-mixed spirits.

By December, reports from Merrydown indicated that they were hoping for a takeover bid. They had lost £94 000 in the six months up to September 1997 compared with a profit of £673 000 in the year before. When their chairman stood down after 32 years, he said that Two Dogs sales had collapsed. The market had been flooded by more than 90 new products and the effect had been cataclysmic.

AND AFTERWARDS?

Experimentation with alcopops and new health drinks continued (*The Guardian* 16 June 1998) and Portman's repeated reprimands to brewers for the packaging and advertising of new products in the alcopops line. Evidently all was not completely lost!

The September 1998 Mintel report, 18 months on from the original ecstatic coverage of alcopops, is more measured. It presents the forecasts given earlier in this case from 1998 and reports that Hooch was still a strong brand representing 85% of the market with a sound niche market, though not as booming as first predicted. It reports on Hooch's continuing marketing flair: their introduction of special edition flavours at Christmas and on St Valentine's Day, "Hoo La La" for the World Cup and Hoopers Reef for the more mature market.

Hooch had also had a strong export strategy since 1996. All in all it represents 10% of Bass's turnover by value. Merrydown was still in the market and exporting strongly to continental Europe while Whitbread launched Shott's in Ireland at the end of 1997.

However, the market has calmed down. On the whole the report attributes this to

- The fact that people are still unhappy about the target (over half interviewed respondents still say "these products encourage under-age drinking" when asked)
- Retailers are still pulling out
- The cost of market entry in terms of product development and marketing cost is high

In summary:

> The factors which were brought to bear on the market which contributed to its early success (even the bad publicity, which helped generate huge awareness of the new product), have also helped contribute to sales decline. (Mintel 1998)

The main target group – the 18–24-year-olds – want to be seen with a more sophisticated drink . . . any new product will need to be backed by product and/or advertising spend and have extensive distribution.

Questions

1. Look at the general picture for alcohol consumption in different European countries; what were the particular strengths and weaknesses of the British alcohol market in 1995? How do alcopops fit in?
2. If you had aimed to be the leading brand in the alcopops market in 1995, what measures would you have taken? What would you regard as the most important points of development of your brand?

3. How far do you think you could have used negative publicity to increase sales amongst your target group?
4. Outline the ethical issues here? Do you think they were well founded?
5. Do you regard this case as the story of a craze which has gone as soon as it peaked, or a success story for Hooch?
6. The news in February 1999 carried an item about the problem of additives in cigarettes which could appeal to children. Vanilla and coconut were mentioned. Many additives are currently used. Imagine you are in charge of brand development for your cigarette company and make a plan for the next two years.

References and further reading

REPORTS

BRMB (September 1996) Levels of usage of alcopops and consumer attitudes towards them. Mintel.
Euromonitor (September 1995) Market focus, Alcoholic drinks.
Euromonitor (May 1996) Market focus, Alcoholic Carbonates.
Hamon, A. (July 1997) Alcopops consumption: age issues. Unpublished MSc, July.
Mintel (March 1997) Alcoholic soft drinks. Market Intelligence.
Mintel (September 1998) Alcoholic Soft Drinks. Mintel.
Zenith (November 1994) Guide to Sports Drinks in Europe.

NEWSPAPER ARTICLES

Birmingham Post, 12 May 1997 (on alcopops and liver failure in children).
The Guardian, 17 January 1997 – "Alcopops" a hit with young.
The Guardian, 16 June 1998 (on the rise of energy drinks).
The Independent, 18 July 1997 – Teenage "alcocops" to spy on shops.
The Independent, 8 August 1997 – Brewers take a fresh look at the alcopops market.
The Independent, 28 August 1997 – Five alcopops withdrawn from sale: Drink.
Marketing Week, 18 September 1997 (reports on first fall in sales of alcopops May/June).
The Times, 31 January 1996 – Beer is for bores as the market goes pop.

16

Kruszgeo: who are its customers?

Krysztof Przybylowski

Case	Business-to-business marketing
Main focus	Buying criteria, product development processes
Subsidiary focus	Reverse marketing, vertical integration
Scene	Poland, Europe
Players	Gravel manufacturers, concrete manufacturers
Product	Gravel

Summary

The success of many building and construction contractors in Poland depends on their continuing supply of high quality gravel, a major ingredient of the concrete they use. Kruszgeo, an employee-owned firm, produces such gravel. What would be Kruszgeo's best strategies, in terms of dealing with customers in their different products? In particular, should they buy a firm which produces and sells concrete?

© 2000 John Wiley & Sons, Ltd.
Understanding Marketing: A European Casebook edited by Celia Phillips, Ad Pruyn and Marie-Paule Kestemont.

Introduction

This industrial marketing case looks at a commodity without which Poland (and indeed any twentieth century economy) cannot expand – gravel. It is unlikely that most readers will have given this product, a thought – they may well have classified it up to now, along with air and water, as a natural part of their environment. However, the construction world is more complicated than that. Gravel has to be refined – cleaned and graded by size – in order to make a reliable concrete which in turn will form the basis of the construction industry and its roads and buildings. It is in fact a crucial product which needs stringent production processes – the product manufacturing process is key.

Apart from these technical aspects of product marketing, we are asked to think about the organization of companies which produce gravel, and in particular Kruszgeo, a gravel producer in southeast Poland. Given the stages of production – from gravel to cement – before the finished product is used in building, what are the arguments for and against "integrating forward" – buying up a concrete manufacturing firm – to maximize profits?

Readers should also note that Kruszgeo, having been privatized along with most Polish businesses in the last few years, is now employee-owned. All in all, this is a thought-provoking short case, which enables readers to think about a common set of industrial marketing problems in an unfamiliar context.

KEYWORDS

Industrial marketing, organizational decision process, buying centre, buying criteria.

Case

Somewhat curiously, success for many contractors serving the booming Polish building and highway construction market depends on the continuing supply of the high quality gravel which goes into the concrete they sell. Kruszgeo, an employee-owned firm in Rzeszow, produces gravel for contractors and construction firms in southeastern Poland. The case asks the student to be a consultant to Kruszgeo's president and to try to assess the buying situation for two segments of the firm's customers: (1) concrete block and stone producers and (2) readymix concrete producers. The case also asks the student to assess the advantages and disadvantages of "integrating forward" and having Kruszgeo actually buy a firm which produces and sells concrete.

GRAVEL IS GRAVEL IS GRAVEL! OR IS IT?

Gravel, the humble commodity we all take for granted, is essential if the rocketing construction boom throughout Poland is to continue. The sources of gravel demand in Poland are very similar to these in East Germany. The urgent necessity to refurbish almost all East German cities and the need to build thousands of kilometres of new highways generates an enormous demand for gravel.

SOME ABCS OF GRAVEL AND CONCRETE

First of all gravel is unconsolidated; it is a natural accumulation of rock fragments resulting from erosion, consisting predominantly of particles larger than sand (diameter greater than 2 mm), such as boulders, cobbles, pebbles, granules, or any other combination of these. Secondly, it might surprise many outsiders that not all gravel is the same. That fact is very important for the industry. As a component of concrete, gravel has two critical dimensions:

- The size and cleanliness of the gravel. Clean and correct sized gravel improves the quality of the resulting concrete – and avoids the quality problems plaguing some Polish concrete producers whose concrete chips and cracks unnecessarily.
- The nature of the gravel, natural versus crushed. Companies in northeastern and southwestern Poland typically produce natural gravel, the kind most suitable for construction purposes. Other areas of Poland, in particular the south, often produce crushed gravel, which is suitable for highway construction but not building construction.

Concrete production usually takes one of three forms:

- Manufacture of hard-concrete products like blocks and stones.
- Concrete production right at the construction site.
- Production of readymix concrete in mixing trucks for just-in-time delivery to construction sites. Production of one cubic metre of readymix concrete requires about 1200 kilograms of gravel, 700 kilograms of sand, and 300 kilograms of cement.

An advantage of producing hard-concrete blocks and stones is that because they can be stored, the firm can stabilize production more easily and avoid the wide seasonal fluctuations which are typical for countries like Poland or Germany.

THE POLISH MARKET

Precise estimates of the size of the Polish concrete market are difficult to come by. With the building boom in Warsaw, the Polish capital represents the largest single-city market in Poland – about one-third of the country's total readymix concrete market. During the next couple of years other large Polish cities will follow Warsaw. The consumption of readymix concrete for all Poland in 1996 was estimated to be about 2 million cubic metres. In following years two-figure growth is expected.

Huge as the 1996 market was – both in euros and volume terms – the gravel and concrete markets in Poland are expected to expand significantly in the near future, as noted before. Two forces are driving the expansion, the continuing demand for concrete in building construction and the imminent takeoff in road construction expected throughout Poland. The cost of Polish road construction alone in the next 12–15 years is expected to reach 10 billion euros. The construction industry in Poland will be further boosted by the rise in demand for housing construction and housing refurbishing. In order for the cement companies to remain in business and meet these demands, they have to ensure their own supply of gravel. This is an absolute necessity for them. A reliable supply of quality gravel makes it possible for the cement company to produce quality concrete – the backbone of its sales and profits – and to reduce its production and marketing risks. (Bad materials in this case will lead to dangerous and public failures in products.)

PRIVATIZING THE GRAVEL PRODUCERS

Concrete producers across Poland watched and participated in the privatization process of dozens of gravel firms throughout 1996 and 1997. Owing to the cost of transportation the most attractive gravel extracting companies were those located near major Polish cities and industrial areas such as:

- Olsztyn Mines of Industrial Minerals (OKSM) – serves mostly the Warsaw region and northeastern Poland
- Zielona Gôra Mines of Industrials Mineral (ZKSM) – serves western Poland and East Germany
- Wrocław Mines of Industrial Minerals (WKSM) – serves mostly the Wrocław region and East Germany
- Köslan Mines of Industrial Minerals (KSMK) – serves central Poland, Lódź region
- Kielce Mines of Industrial Minerals (KKSM) – serves southern Poland, Kielce region
- Cracow Corporation of Industrial Minerals Extraction (KZEK) – serves the Cracow region

All these firms have both Polish and Western European suitors in the privatization process. Western European concrete producers interested in the Polish companies include firms from Germany, France, Belgium, Britain, Denmark and Ireland. While these companies welcome the cash infusions that new owners can bring, the Polish Treasury Ministry did not want any single foreign firm to have complete ownership of one of these gravel producers and limited such dominant equity investments. In addition, some cement and concrete producers tried to limit their gravel-supply problems by integrating backward and buying up gravel producers.

MARKETING ISSUES

But not all gravel firms are searching for new capital from foreign investors. One such firm is Kruszgeo, an employee-owned firm located in Rzeszow. The dominant gravel producer in southeast Poland, Kruszgeo had 1995 annual sales of well over a million euros. In order to maintain its position and ensure future development the managers at Kruszgeo must thoroughly understand their customers' buying criteria. This is often called reverse marketing because the buyer specifies all the buying criteria and the transaction takes place if the seller can meet or exceed them.

The most important buying criteria for Kruszgeo customers will be:

- The price of the gravel
- The meeting of quality and technical specifications for the gravel
- Company reputation in meeting the delivery schedules
- Claim policies in case the product proves to be of poor quality

The clients will also consider

- Production facilities and production capacity.

Companies who used to buy gravel from Kruszgeo before will be able to make a decision fairly quickly thanks to the past experience since the buying situation is a straight rebuy. For new customers the decision to buy gravel will be far more complex. They will have to assess Kruszgeo's potential to meet their buying criteria. That task will be the responsibility of a number of client company employees with different kinds of expertise – called the buying centre. It is critical for the sales manager at Kruszgeo to identify people at concrete producer companies who have influence on the gravel buying process (Bristor 1993). These roles differ from industry to industry and company to company. Gravel orders are usually large volume, and contracted for long periods. In practice this means that large sums of money are involved. These factors influence the structure of buying centres among companies producing concrete.

Assume that Jan Wilczek, Kruszgeo's president, believes that his company faces critical marketing decisions in two areas:

- Identifying effective ways to sell to various segments of concrete producers
- Deciding whether to "integrate forward" to buy a cement producer so Kruszgeo can actually sell concrete to its subsidiary company.

He calls you in as a consultant to advise the company. Looking at the situation, you recognize the special complexities of firms like Kruszgeo which sell industrial products; they sell products for which a derived demand exists. In Kruszgeo's case demand for its gravel is derived from the demand for its customers' concrete that, in turn, is derived from the demand for the buildings and highways their customers ask them to construct. In your analysis you realize the vital importance of understanding what Kruszgeo's customers' customers want and set about studying that issue. In the process of your consulting work, you focus your efforts on the three questions below.

Questions

1. Consider the buying situation for a prospective customer for Kruszgeo which produces concrete blocks and stones. Identify (a) what individuals might be in this firm's "buying centre" for this purchase, (b) what buying criteria the buying centre members might use and which one or two are most likely to be critical, and (c) marketing actions that Kruszgeo might use to make a successful sale to the prospective customer.
2. Now consider the buying situation for a prospective Kruszgeo customer which delivers its readymix concrete to a contractor's construction site. Identify (a) what individuals might be in this firm's "buying centre", (b) what buying criteria they might use and which are likely to be most critical, and (c) marketing actions Kruszgeo might use to make a successful sale to this prospective customer.
3. What are the major advantages and disadvantages for Kruszgeo in integrating forward and buying a firm that actually produces and sells concrete?

References and further reading

Bristor, J.M. (1993) Influence strategies in organizational buying: The importance of connections to the right people in the right places. *Journal of Business-to-Business Marketing*, 1: 55–61.

Stepien, T. (1996) Grabbing for gravel. *Warsaw Business Journal* (November 1, I-17), pp. 1, 16, 17.

The Economist (1997) Survey Business in Eastern Europe. (November 22nd), pp. 6–22.

Warsaw School of Economics (1998) *Poland International Economic Report 1997/98*. Warsaw.

17

ZTM: a public transportation system

Krysztof Przybylowski

Case	Marketing distribution and sales
Main focus	Pricing strategy, distribution system
Subsidiary focus	Break-even analysis
Scene	Warsaw
Players	Local government, retail outlets, passengers
Product	Tickets

Summary

Warsaw's City Transportation Board has increased the price of single-ride tickets for public transportation in an attempt to increase the percentage of passengers buying extended-duration tickets. However, such tickets give the kiosk owners who sell them very small profit margins. They are reluctant to cooperate. How can they be encouraged to do so?

Introduction

The reader is presented here with a nice cautionary tale about distribution. An important strategic decision has been made at the highest level about a public city transportation system – it must stop running at a loss. To this end, and in particular to encourage passengers to buy tickets, rather than travel illegally without them, a new ticketing pricing structure is introduced. Reactions from the travelling public are disappointing because it is almost impossible for them to find a retailer who will provide the new ticket! This is a classic illustration of the effects of having different layers of marketing management in an organization where the strategy decided at the highest level has not been worked through to its execution.

The idea is an interesting one, and readers are given ample information to attempt to solve the problem for themselves. This exercise should prove a useful tool for helping in the understanding of retail distribution and the implementation of a pricing strategy.

KEYWORDS

Pricing strategy, pricing objectives, break-even analysis.

Case

CITY TRANSPORTATION BOARD (ZTM)

Warsaw, the capital of Poland with a population of almost two million people, is the largest city in Poland. It is comparable with Budapest and Prague and is about four times smaller than Paris or London. Like any other big city, it suffers from typical problems resulting from urbanization. One of them lies in its transportation system, which is rather underdeveloped in comparison with those of the capital cities in neighbouring countries. The difference in terms of transportation infrastructure is even bigger if you compare Warsaw to Amsterdam or Barcelona. Solutions to such problems are decided at the highest national level, namely the Polish Parliament and

Government. However, a number of issues can only be solved at the level of local government and even at the level of companies owned by the Warsaw local government authority.

A major difficulty Warsaw has to face lies in the decreasing number of passengers using public transport. This is made up of buses, trams and subway, all of which are managed by ZTM and use the same tickets for all services. This trend seems to be typical in all European cities. For example, between 1993 and 1995 the total number of passengers carried by GVB buses, the Amsterdam public transportation company, decreased from 56.7 million to 51.7 million (Halaba 1997). The situation was the same for all public transport in Amsterdam: GVB trams, buses, night buses, and metro carried 253.7 million passengers in 1993 but only 237.0 million in 1995. The main reason is that more and more passengers prefer to drive their own vehicles rather than using public transport. Taxis are not regarded as a realistic alternative as they are relatively expensive. In these terms Warsaw is no different. Warsaw City Hall would like to stop that tendency and if possible reverse it. In order to achieve that goal it is essential to undertake several marketing actions that would stem from the Warsaw public transportation company having a consistent marketing strategy. The real challenge is to find a proper combination of marketing mix strategies. The most urgent issues to be solved are those of ticket pricing, ticket distribution and the need for more passengers to use extended-duration tickets.

"We estimate that the percentage of people who will use extended-duration tickets will increase [from 60%] to about 70%," said Andrzej Wisniewski, City Transportation Board (ZTM) press spokesman. Wisniewski is referring to ZTM's decision to raise single ticket prices for Warsaw public transportation by 40%. The increase is huge but Poles are accustomed to such dramatic changes in prices. The shock was not expected to last long. The monthly passes, however, will increase by only 12.5%, and many other multi-ride ticket options will be introduced which will make it much more economical for the frequent public transport user to buy extended-duration tickets.

But is this strategy really going to streamline operations and smooth out bumps in the cash flow, as ZTM hopes it will? There are some good signs that it could work well in Warsaw since it works well, for example, in Barcelona. The single-journey ticket for all means of public transport in Barcelona costs 145 pesetas (about 0.9 Euros), whereas the price for ten trips is 795 pesetas and for a monthly pass 5450 pesetas. Will Warsaw passengers favour similar solutions to their counterparts in Barcelona?

ZTM'S OBJECTIVE IN RAISING TICKET PRICES

In Warsaw's case the change has to be broadened. First of all it is necessary to increase ticket prices. Wisniewski expects the fare increase to bring in 311 million zloty (about 78 million Euros) in revenue to ZTM in 1997, which would be a 20% increase over 1996. This zl.311 million accounts for about two-thirds of the overall 1997 budget of zl.440 million; the remainder of the budget should come from city subsidies. However, the budget only covers operating expenses, not investments. For instance, in 1996, ZTM took out a zl.88 million loan from Bank Przemyslowo-Handlowy to upgrade its ailing fleet of buses. "We are considering an additional loan to be underwritten this year, also for the transport fleet," said Wisniewski.

The company is also hoping that an increase in the purchase of extended-use passes will decrease its losses, estimated at zl.40 million annually, from non-paying users. More choices which carry obvious consumer savings compared with single-use tickets should lure many into buying tickets rather than facing penalties, Wisniewski reasons. Also these actions could be supplemented by some promotional activities, such as competitions that encourage people to buy tickets and thus decrease the number of non-paying passengers, and these are being planned.

Current methods of dealing with fare avoidance involve the use of ticket inspectors (authorized controllers). They are not uniformed, but wear badges and carry identification which they are required to show to passengers when carrying out their random inspections.

There are several drawbacks with the system:

- Few inspections are carried out at night because of security problems
- Fraud

The deterrent for non-payers is a fine of about 100 times the fare, and the system is open to abuse. Passengers found avoiding fares may either send the fine directly to ZTM by post or banking transfer, or they can pay the controller directly. In either case, it is almost impossible to check.

Both these problems give the inspection service difficulties with its public relations and inspectors are frequently accused of bribery and suffer violence.

How can the new ideas be translated into action?

THE NEW WARSAW PUBLIC TRANSPORTATION RATES AND CONSUMER REACTIONS

The price for a single ticket to use the bus will increase from zl.1 to zl.1.40, while the price for a monthly pass will only increase from zl.39.44 to zl. 45. In addition, passengers will be able to purchase a one-day pass for zl.4 to be used within Warsaw city limits, or zl.6 to be used outside the city borders. A ticket allowing three months of unlimited use will be priced at zl.130 and six-month tickets at zl.260, A one-day pass for two adults and three children will cost zl.8, and a weekend group ticket for five people will cost zl.14.

Surprisingly, reaction reported in the press by the public to the rate increases has been positive, and many public transport users are planning to switch to extended-use passes because of the increases. "Now I am going to use a monthly ticket," said Halina Snopkiewicz, a pensioner, punching a single-use ticket while riding a downtown tram. Zofia Duda, 68, said she would stick with monthly tickets although the rate increase is "a serious burden for my pension. I travel a lot and monthly tickets are the most convenient," she added.

So, from the consumer's viewpoint, it seems the strategy will be a success – consumers are being weaned off the single-use tickets, are not upset by the price increases, and find the extended-use passes more convenient. Tadeusz Lapinski, owner of a kiosk on Pulawska Street with 14 years in the business reports, "Several years ago I used to sell up to 3000 single tickets per week. Now I only sell between five and six hundred."

THE DISTRIBUTION SYSTEM AND ADEQUATE MARGINS FOR DISTRIBUTORS

ZTM's actual ticket distribution system may be the company's biggest weakness. Because of rush hour crushes, it is not possible to buy tickets on the buses and ZTM operates only 40 ticket sales outlets throughout the whole city, located mainly at the bus and tram termini, as well as an outlet at the company headquarters in Warsaw downtown, and two other temporary downtown outlets which are one kilometre away. Most ticket sales are made through the major press distributors, including Ruch SA and Jard Press. They sell the tickets wholesale to kiosk owners, who in turn sell them retail to the public. Almost all the kiosk owners sell single-ride tickets: only 50% of the 830 kiosks served by Ruch SA and 10% of the 600 to 700 kiosks served by Jard Press sell multi-ride tickets.

If the majority of the kiosk owners, the primary distributors, are not selling the extended-use passes, as reported above, then the sales growth in these tickets will not be as high as ZTM would like (and seems to expect). The kiosk owners are reluctant to sell these passes because of the slim margin on returns. For a single-use ticket, the kiosk owners receive a 5% margin, whereas they only receive a 1% margin on multi-ride passes.

This slim margin results from the leasing system in place. Kiosk owners are required to lease ZTM's official stamp for zl.50 in order to stamp a date on the multi-ride passes. When the kiosk owners sell 5000 or more monthly tickets per month (zl.200 000 in sales), they are also required to buy VAT-receipt cash registers for a price of zl.5000. "After I bought the register and the stamp, it was like selling the tickets for free for more than three months," says Lapinski (a kiosk owner).

Safety is also a major concern for the kiosk owners because of the current delivery and payment system. The kiosk owners buy the single-use tickets from the press distributors at a discount and then sell them to the public, while extended-use passes are sold on a commission basis. This means the extended-use passes can sit for up to two weeks before they are sold in the relatively unsecured streetside kiosks, "The number of monthly tickets each kiosk owner can have varies from one hundred to several thousand," says Teresa

Kalota, ticket sales manager with Jard Press. "In the case of the largest sellers, it might amount to hundreds of thousands of zlotys." Lapinski, the kiosk owner on Pulawska Street says ". . . the profit we get from the sales of monthly tickets is too small to bother."

Unless ZTM alters its pricing strategy to facilitate its distribution system, consumers will not have adequate access to the extended-use passes through the kiosk vending system.

Questions

1. Look at the new price structure for single tickets, monthly passes, three-month tickets and six-month tickets. (a) What are the advantages and disadvantages of this "price lining" strategy for (1) ZTM, (2) kiosk operators and (3) passengers? (b) How would you set these prices? (c) What would the impact be on ZTM's three stakeholder groups mentioned in (a)?
2. What pricing strategy should ZTM develop to increase kiosk distribution of extended use tickets?
3. Assume that the kiosk operators receive 20% of the retail price of single tickets and 4% of the retail price of monthly passes as payment from ZTM for selling the products. (a) What would the monthly sales revenue be for selling only the single tickets or only the monthly passes at these volumes: 500, 1000, 1500, 2000? (b) Considering these revenues and the case information, what are the advantages and disadvantages for the kiosk operators of selling (1) only single tickets or (2) only monthly passes?
4. Assume the unit variable cost of carrying each of the tickets (single tickets and extended-use tickets) is 50% of the commission received for the single tickets and 20% for the monthly passes. Under the new pricing structure, how many (a) single tickets and (b) monthly passes would a kiosk vender have to sell to pay for its purchase of the VAT-receipt cash register and its lease of the official stamp?
5. Suggest other means by which tickets could be distributed and discuss their advantages and disadvantages.
6. Compare transport marketing as described here with that in other European cities with which you are familiar.

References and further reading

Halaba, M. (1997) Ticket to ride. *Warsaw Business Journal* (January 27–February 2), pp. 1, 21.
<http://infoseek.go.com/WebDir/Travel/Transportation/>
<http://www.nationalexpress.co.uk/>
www.tmb.net/eng/titols/tars.htm

18

NIVEA: brand transfer for continuous and innovative product maintenance

Alexander Roosdorp

Case	Product management
Main focus	Brand extensions, brand transfer
Subsidiary focus	Positioning model, communication
Scene	Germany, worldwide
Players	Beiersdorf, consumers
Product	Cosmetics

Summary

Brand transfer is the central element of product maintenance for NIVEA. Numerous new and successful products under the brand name NIVEA and the long tradition of the classic NIVEA creams indicate the importance of both continuity and innovative product maintenance. The case shows how NIVEA has managed to combine the apparent differences of traditional and modern products with a successful strategy of product maintenance.

Understanding Marketing: A European Casebook edited by Celia Phillips, Ad Pruyn and Marie-Paule Kestemont.

Introduction

Like Case 4, this case also has NIVEA as its subject matter. This time the arena is one of product management.

The writer takes a saturated market – the German home market – and shows how Beiersdorf uses its main brand (which is a major player in the skin food market) to increase its market share for related products such as body lotions. The German body-care market is introduced and Beiersdorf "cosmed's" main competitors evaluated. The idea of product maintenance through brand transfer the NIVEA way is then described. NIVEA cream has always been regarded as the embodiment of "nourishment" and "mildness" and these characteristics must underpin new brand extensions and in particular the first, "nourishment". NIVEA is also seen as

- High quality
- Value for money
- Unfussy
- Having good distribution
- Not primarily having a medical concept

These characteristics are also used as concepts in advertising and product development for the new extension brands. The advantages of this are clear – NIVEA has little extra work to do in this area – the images are well-honed and understood by millions.

In order to grow further, however, Beiersdorf cosmed needs more products. The case for brand "transfer" (rather than mere "extension") in a product maintenance programme is discussed. The analysis forecasts successive stages in the introduction of sub-brands

- *Market analysis* – here positioning and pricing are important
- *The filling of sub-markets* – to "spoil" the opposition
- *Advertising* – for both new and established products
- *Dealing with high risk innovations*

Beginning from this exposition, readers are led to questions on the problems which Beiersdorf might face through using such a strategy, the limits to brand transfer, advertising challenges and the types of market research needed.

KEYWORDS

Product maintenance, brand transfer, brand extension, brand core, positioning model, growth strategy, conversion measures, integrated communication.

Case

THE BEIERSDORF COMPANY AND THE NIVEA BRAND

The Beiersdorf company has three areas of business. These are shown in Figure 18.1.

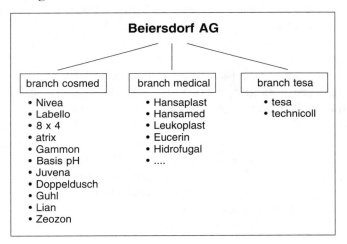

FIGURE 18.1   The branch organization of Beiersdorf AG. Source: in-house material.

"Cosmed" is Beiersdorf's main earner and accounts for 53.2% of business area revenue. Beiersdorf medical, representing 24.1% of the group's revenue in 1999, comprises the areas of medical skin treatment and nourishment under the brands Hansaplast, Eucerin, Hidrofugal and so forth. The area "tesa" is represented in the adhesive tape market within both the consumer and the industrial markets with its brand tesa.

In 1996 Beiersdorf "cosmed" achieved revenues of approximately DM3 billion (about 1.54 billion Euros), a growth of 5.7% over the previous year. The revenues of this branch are still mainly generated by the German home market (DM1.08 billion), although the international business has become increasingly important. Its traditional brand, NIVEA, is the strongest brand within the Beiersdorf AG. In spite of saturated, highly competitive markets NIVEA achieved two-figure growth in revenues for five years in succession and gained market leadership. With a revenue of nearly DM2.3 billion it is the largest "body-nourishment" brand in the world. NIVEA's revenue growth in Germany is 10.6% over 1996, compared with 13.3% for the rest of Europe.

NIVEA was introduced to the market in 1911 and was the first cream ever based on a stable water–fat emulsion – an invention which revolutionized the cosmetics industry. The word "Nivea" was derived from Latin and means something like "snowy". From the point of view of product maintenance it is particularly important that the composition of the cream has not been significantly changed since its invention. The typical blue and white tin box was introduced in 1925. Up to the beginning of the 1980s, the cream accounted for 50% of the NIVEA brand revenues. Since the beginning of the 1970s systematic line extensions have increasingly contributed to total NIVEA revenues and growth. Through subsequent brand transfer NIVEA has been developed from being solely a skin cream brand to being a "holding brand" for body nourishment products. In spite of the current product innovation and new sub-brands the classic cream could retain a small increase in revenues and still dominates the skin cream market with a 30% market share.

THE GERMAN BODY-CARE MARKET

The market for body nourishment – and cosmetic products – is highly competitive, and in many countries, saturated. Since Germany is NIVEA's most important market and also a highly saturated one, it will be analysed in more detail in the following.

Beiersdorf competes with Procter & Gamble, Unilever and L'Oréal, all of which are many times larger. In spite of this, the "cosmed" area has successfully managed to maintain its market leadership in its relevant product category – nourishment and cosmetic markets –

with approximately 20% of the market share. Details are given in Figure 18.2.

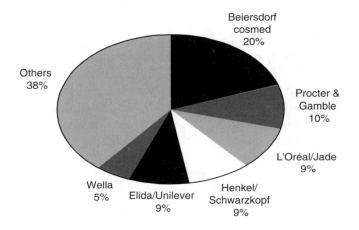

FIGURE 18.2   Group market shares in the German body-care and cosmetic market in 1995. Source: Nielsen, in Beiersdorf (1996), p. 45.

The body-care and cosmetic market is arranged as follows:

- Skin care
- Facial care
- Lip care
- Sun protection
- Men's cosmetics

- Deodorants
- Bath/shower
- Soaps
- Hair-care
- Women's scents

The single competitors have different activities within these areas, and for this reason market shares can vary. The "holding brand" NIVEA achieves market leadership in many of these market segments with specific sub-brands such as NIVEA Visage, NIVEA Sun and so forth.

PRODUCT MAINTENANCE THROUGH SYSTEMATIC BRAND TRANSFER

Beiersdorf AG applies a sub-branding model with NIVEA, which associates continuity and innovation under the holding brand NIVEA.

NIVEA creme, which has been successful for over 80 years, embodies the unchanged brand core of "nourishment" and "mildness". In spite of some new introductions like hair-milk, shampoo, bath soap and so forth, the classic cream was the only really successful product well into the 1970s. It was not until the decision was made to initiate systematic assortment extensions and a brand transfer from the brand for skin cream to a holding brand for skin nourishment, that the long-term success of other NIVEA products was made possible.

Strict rules underlie the development and introduction of new NIVEA brands. NIVEA products must represent the "nourishment version" in all future markets and in comparison with competition (Prick 1989). Furthermore, the basic benefit of the brand (high quality, reasonable price, simplicity, wide distribution, and the fact that it is not a medical product targeted at different skin types) needs to be fulfilled. The current introduction of new products is thus controlled through the systematic positioning model shown in Figure 18.3.

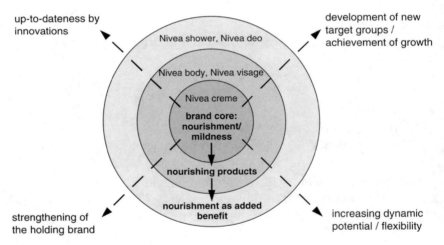

up-to-dateness by innovations

development of new target groups / achievement of growth

Nivea shower, Nivea deo

Nivea body, Nivea visage

Nivea creme

brand core: nourishment/ mildness

nourishing products

nourishment as added benefit

strengthening of the holding brand

increasing dynamic potential / flexibility

FIGURE 18.3   NIVEA's positioning model. Source: in-house material.

Around the brand core of NIVEA creme we find all the nourishing products such as "NIVEA body" or "visage". In an outer "circle", somewhat further from the core, the other sub-brands are located, which offer nourishment as an additional but not main benefit

("NIVEA shower", "bath" and so forth). The NIVEA brand achieves the following advantages by applying this systematic division of core brands and sub-brands:

- "Up-to-dateness" through innovation
- The development of new target groups and consequent achievement of growth
- Increasing dynamic potential concerning brand management and flexibility of product maintenance
- Strengthening of the holding brand

For NIVEA, innovation explicitly means that the products are continuously (proactively) adapted to the environment. For NIVEA sub-brands this adaptation process consists of relaunches, or the introduction of new sub-brands. Changes in the classic cream, on the other hand, are not noticed by consumers at first glance (for instance, changes in the consistency). The reason for this distinction lies in the customer benefit that is being addressed. The more specific the benefit of a product (as is the case with the sub-brands), the more innovative and modern the product must be. "Skin nourishment", the general benefit bestowed by NIVEA creme, scarcely varies, and because of this does not require constant product improvements. The brand core is therefore retained unchanged. This continuity of all (new) products contributes to the continuous strengthening of the brand.

CONVERSION MEASURES FOR SUCCESSFUL PRODUCT MAINTENANCE

Systematic market analysis and introduction

The systematic introduction of sub-brands is of great importance for NIVEA. The following four points describe methods which have been successfully used by NIVEA brands and benefits.

Systematic and encompassing analysis phase The process always passes through three important, but in this business often neglected, phases:

- Extensive market research will help clarify the main shopping factors for the new product. We can then estimate the most sensible retail outlets for the new product segment.
- The existing competitors in this business area are analysed in depth (chance-risk analysis).
- Based on these market analyses NIVEA's positioning gap is defined (or not, if there is none). Emphasis is put on the question as to whether or not this new market and its challenges fit NIVEA's positioning. This is to guarantee that NIVEA's positioning is strengthened continuously and in the long run, and that the brand value increases.

NIVEA is a follower, not an innovator   NIVEA does not claim to be the market innovator. New developments and trends are always first observed and examined, to see whether they will be suitable in the long run. On the other hand, NIVEA is the brand that normally first manages to offer an innovation in a convincing price/performance ratio and in this way establishes the market from the point of view of revenue. NIVEA's innovation capacity lies in the fact that its product quality is at least as good as the luxury brands – the innovators – but at a much lower price.

Concentration on strategically important sub-brands   For NIVEA the area of facial care is unmistakably the most important, because in this sub-market innovations are developed, and the face, considered a sensitive and cosmetically important area of the body, is ideal for the positioning of "nourishment and mildness". Through massive activities in this field, the NIVEA brand can be certain to leave an innovative impression(NIVEA must be a leader in this product area in order to pick up consumer trends and new developments as early as possible, and to be the first to establish these new markets.)

Price–performance relationship as the basic element   The quality of the products does not need to shy away from a comparison with luxury brands. NIVEA realizes that it can change the rules of the market and set its prices far below those of the luxury brands. In addition, thanks to its well-known and understood product range and clear positioning, NIVEA offers consumers security in a market that is flooded with numerous product varieties.

Filling important sub-markets to limit competition

Well-aimed line extensions within its sub-brands make it possible for NIVEA to secure and develop market leadership for its core products. Because the characteristics of the products within the NIVEA brand comprise almost the entire market and represent a clear and "need oriented" standard (nourishment, mildness, good quality at a fair price), competitors find it difficult to acquire market shares, especially because the product variants of NIVEA hardly cannibalize each other. NIVEA limits itself to relatively few products, each of which is believable in itself and provides the consumer with a sensibly differentiated product. Figure 18.4 shows the impressive share of the market NIVEA has gained through differentiated sub-brands. It has strengthened its position still further with this strategy.

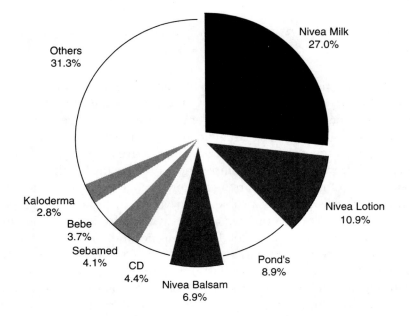

FIGURE 18.4   Market shares in body lotions: Germany 1995. Source: Nielsen, in Beiersdorf (1996), p. 54.

Exploitation of synergy effects in the market communication

The dilemma of having a market adaptation that is both as differentiated and as integrated as possible has already been mentioned. In this context it must be noted that advertising is the chief instrument in the business. In order to achieve its apparently contradictory goals, NIVEA concentrates its advertising efforts on the new products, but nevertheless does not neglect the holding brand NIVEA. This is achieved by a homogeneous appearance in campaigns or well-aimed image advertising. The brand's basic values must be continuously recharged (keywords: first-in-mind, continuity) but demonstrate its innovation power. The core brand guarantees continuity, whereas the numerous innovations (at least one new product every three months) stand for up-to-dateness. Only by selective advertising for the new products and by "neglecting" the older products can the sub-brands be sufficiently differentiated on a limited budget.

Limitation to higher risk innovations in segments with small revenues

A fundamental risk of brand transfer is that efforts could be directed to short-lived trends. The damages to the positioning often turn out to be higher than the increase in revenues which can be generated in the short run. In NIVEA's case it can sometimes happen that the company must react to such trends, creating corresponding products, in order to show innovation competence, in particular in the smaller sub-markets. Only a few years ago, there was a trend in facial care products towards gel. The problem for NIVEA in the use of the gel arose from the fact it mainly consisted of water and that the nourishment aspect therefore did not fit its positioning. In spite of this, NIVEA developed and marketed two rival products. The trend towards gel products did not last long, and revenues started to decline again. Since these products, from the point of view of the entire NIVEA range, only represented a small portion of NIVEA revenues, they had little effect on consumers' image perception, and the "damage" caused by a lack of continuity was irrelevant.

CONCLUSIONS

NIVEA's holding brand strategy, with its basic line extension idea, is its chief instrument for product maintenance. The typical problems of product maintenance in this business can be seen as a lack of continuity and/or up-to-dateness of positioning. These two requirements can be seen both as important problems and as goal dimensions for NIVEA. They are assured by a comprehensive positioning model, which defines the context for further sub-brands. In addition, clear principles guide brand transfer. These are: independence in the sub-markets, a recognizable added benefit within the area "nourishment/mildness", an uncomplicated character, no need to solve complicated technical problems, quality leadership, perceived "value for money" and, of course, wide distribution.

Questions

1. What difficulties do you think NIVEA will face in their efforts to boost performance levels by introducing brand transfer? What critical success factors exist? How should NIVEA proceed, to best exploit existing potential?
2. What prerequisites must exist, so that market research results in the successful evaluation of new products? What suitable methods of market research can be used for this purpose?
3. How do you assess NIVEA's future potential for expansion by using brand transfer? Where does the potential for growth exist (services, market areas)? Where do limits exist?
4. What problems does the concept of integrated communication cause for NIVEA? What solutions are available? When referring to solutions, go into the whole area between advertising the company's image and the introduction of new products.
5. How would you assess NIVEA's strategy of only introducing high-risk innovative procedures in areas that are not hugely significant in terms of turnover? What are the advantages and disadvantages of this?

References and further reading

Aaker, D.A. (1991) *Managing Brand Equity*. New York: Free Press.
Arnold, D. (1992) *The Hand-book of Management*. Addison-Wesley.
Beiersdorf AG (1996) *Cosmed – Markt und Marken*. Hamburg: Beiersdorf.
Murphy, J.H. (1990) *Brand Strategy*. Englewood Cliffs, NJ: Prentice Hall.
Prick, H.-J. (1989) NIVEA-Markentransfer: Von der Marke für Hautcreme zur Dachmarke für Hautpflege. In: *Markenartikel*, No. 10, pp. 504–509.
Schröter, H.G. (1995) Erfolgsfaktor Marketing: Der Strukturwandel von der Reklame zur Unternehmenssteuerung. Freiberg: Technische Universität Bergakademie Freiberg (Freiberger Arbeitspapiere 95/9).

19

Cumulus: the development of a loyalty card scheme

Thomas Rudolph and Anina Busch

Case	Promotion
Main focus	Database marketing, loyalty cards
Subsidiary focus	Individual information
Scene	Switzerland, France, Germany
Players	Retail and service outlets, consumers
Product	Loyalty card

Summary

On 3 November 1997 Migros, the biggest retailer in Switzerland, introduced its customer card, Cumulus. This introduction and its decisions, problems and challenges are described. Why has Migros introduced a customer loyalty card? How was the Cumulus project treated from conception until its introduction on the entire Swiss market? How does the Cumulus card work and what is the benefit for the customer? What information can be collected by Migros and how can it be used effectively? What are the lessons for those introducing similar schemes?

© 2000 John Wiley & Sons, Ltd.
Understanding Marketing: A European Casebook edited by Celia Phillips,
Ad Pruyn and Marie-Paule Kestemont.

Introduction

This case gives readers an opportunity to look at the marketing potential of introducing a loyalty card scheme. It should prove a useful context for marketing discussions. As this is written (August 1999), Asda, the large UK retailer which has just been taken over by Walmart, the even larger American giant, has announced that it will fund a new price-cutting campaign by abandoning its loyalty card scheme. In a context where Tesco, the current UK market leader, is widely seen to have overtaken Sainsbury, its main rival, through stealing a march in *introducing* the loyalty card, this is bound to give food for thought in marketing circles!

Here, however, we have a large grocery retailing firm, with a large share of the Swiss food and grocery market – nearly a quarter (23.8%) of food products and double its nearest rival. Migros also has interests in many service areas – hotels, restaurants and travel agents are mentioned. Tickets and vouchers for these form part of the loyalty card bonus offer. A further important background factor to the scheme, of which none but Swiss (and neighbouring French and German) readers will probably be aware, lies in the origin of Migros. It began in the 1920s, as its name reflects, as a way of bringing wholesale goods directly to the customer. By 1940 it was a retail cooperative, and as such enjoys a close relationship with its customers. We are told that profit maximization is not its main aim.

Be this as it may, one of the reasons for introducing the Cumulus card in the autumn of 1997 was economic; and the benefits of gathering market information for customer targets and possible savings on the advertising budget are discussed thoroughly. In the context of Migros, the importance for customer bonding is also emphasized. The workings of this specific scheme are described carefully and readers can compare it with schemes nearer home with which they will be more familiar. The discussion questions on this case relate to Migros itself, but can be used to discuss the whole question of the potential advantages and drawbacks of all loyalty schemes both in the short term and in the more problematic, medium view.

KEYWORDS

Customer loyalty, sales promotion, customer individual information, database marketing, direct marketing, customer benefit.

Case

Loyalty cards are a central information and marketing instrument with which market environments may be challenged. They allow companies to improve both customer orientation and customer relations. Loyalty cards are discussed internationally and in different branches of business. Many retailers and service companies in many countries have already introduced or will introduce a loyalty card. Successful and known examples in Europe are the Tesco Club Card, Lufthansa Miles & More, Douglas Card, VW/Audi Card, Ikea Family Plus Card, Superquinn's Superclub Card, etc. On 3 November 1997, Migros, the largest Swiss retail company, launched the customer loyalty card Cumulus.

MIGROS – THE COMPANY

Migros, headquartered in Zurich, was established by Gottlieb Duttweiler in 1925. Duttweiler's vision was to create as direct a link as possible between producers and consumers, so consumers could have a better choice of reasonably priced products. This basic idea is expressed in the name "Migros", which is a combination of the terms "demi" (middle) and "gros" (gross) and stands for "Migros as a distributing organization between wholesale and retail industry". In 1940 Migros was transformed into a retail cooperative. Shares in the cooperative were distributed among consumers and employees. Today the Migros community consists of ten regional cooperatives with approximately 72 000 employees and one and a half million members. This translates into almost half of the households in Switzerland. Because of this tradition and its very popular touch, Migros is part of the Swiss culture and enjoys the confidence and attachment of the Swiss population.

Migros' core business is retailing, divided into food (65% of revenues) and non-food (the remainder) operations. The range of goods comprises approximately 220 000 articles. A special feature of Migros is the fact that 95% of its revenues are generated through the sales of its own label brands which are exclusive to Migros. Migros has several different types of stores. Their main differentiating criteria is the selling space, which determines the range and type of goods offered (M-shops, MM-markets and MMM-shopping centres). In addition, Migros operates specialized discount stores (category killers), speciality stores and M-restaurants. Besides the original retail business, the Migros community has 16 service firms; among these are the Migros-Bank, the Secura-Insurance, the travel organization Hotelplan, and the Migros Club School.

Its core business of retailing accounts for about 80% of total revenues. Migros controls over 580 points of sale in Switzerland. In 1995 Migros experienced stagnation in revenues for the first time in its history because of the general economic climate. Although Migros saw retail revenues of CHF12 700 million (about 7900 million Euros) in 1996, this meant a 1% decline in revenues in comparison with the preceding year. Market shares are as follows:

- Share of total retail volume 16%
- Food share 23.8%
- Non-food share 9.2%

Migros' largest competitor in the retail business is Co-op. In 1996 Co-op reached retail revenues of CHF9048 million, which corresponds to a market share of 13%. In its foreign activities, Migros follows a "border-area" strategy, with points of sale in Germany and France.

Migros' main goal is not necessarily profit maximization. Cultural, social and political goals are as important as economic goals and this stems from its traditions. In order to achieve these goals it has been laid down in the statutes that a given percentage of annual revenues is to be allocated to the achievement of these goals (CHF106.9 million in 1996).

PREREQUISITES AND REASONS FOR INTRODUCING THE CUSTOMER LOYALTY CARD CUMULUS

Economic goals *are* important, however, and to achieve aims such as the consolidation of market leadership, an increase in revenues and a reduction in advertising costs, in a market environment characterized by market saturation, increasing competition and changing consumer behaviour, Migros decided to initiate a customer loyalty programme.

This was known as the Cumulus card. Customers collect points for their purchase at Migros. It was decided such a card offered the following benefits for Migros. It would:

- *Promote customer loyalty and reward the customer*
- *Gain information about the individual needs and habits of customers* – information about shopping frequency and times, shopping basket analysis and store loyalty will help Migros develop closer links with its customers
- *Recognize and exploit cross-selling potentials* – recognition of possibilities for cross-selling will mean that assortment areas with low customer frequency (for instance, furniture and fashion) should profit from areas with high customer frequency (groceries)
- *Communicate more effectively with the customer* by addressing specific customer needs in the medium term through individualized direct advertising campaigns
- *Help make strategic decisions concerning the entire marketing mix in the long run*

In addition, it was hoped that the card would integrate Migros activities in different fields of business within retailing and services and that it could be used to support the entire Migros image.

FROM THE IDEA TO REALITY

An internal project team managed the Cumulus project from its conception to its introduction to the entire Swiss market. In September 1997 the Cumulus card was given to all Migros employees with detailed instructions as to how the card worked as well as a voucher worth CHF25. In October a personalized letter was sent to all cooperative members informing about the Cumulus programme and inviting them to attend promotion events during the introduction. On 3 November 1997 the programme began: the Cumulus loyalty card was officially introduced in Switzerland with an 11-day promotion in every Migros subsidiary. Simultaneously Migros initiated a kick-off advertising campaign: "ready – get set – go and collect Cumulus-points" with full-page and four-colour advertisements in the daily press as well as their own press and posters. The follow-up campaign utilized the same media, but contained other messages. Figure 19.1 shows a typical advertisement.

FIGURE 19.1   Advertisement for Cumulus cards. "Now noodles are turning into bikinis. Start collecting Cumulus points now – and save. Information and Cumulus cards here". Source: Migros, reproduced with their permission.

METHOD AND CUSTOMER BENEFIT OF THE CUMULUS CARD

How does the Cumulus card work?

Obtaining the Cumulus card

Cumulus cards can be obtained at the customer service counters of all M-branches and M-speciality stores. In order to facilitate the immediate use of the card it is attached to the application forms. All family and non-family household members are permitted to collect points on the same account, and to expedite this every participant receives two cards with the same code. To make the collection of Cumulus points even easier for non-frequent household member users the main holder is also given Cumulus stickers with his personal code. In this way Migros seeks to avoid the proliferation of Cumulus cards.

Collecting Cumulus points

For each purchase made in a Migros store, the customer is awarded Cumulus points. Accounts are credited with one Cumulus point for every CHF10 purchase. On specific days, such as a store opening or Saint Valentine's day, points awards are at least doubled. There are also plans to give differential points, awarding customers more points for the purchase of certain products (sales promotion) or shopping at "low frequency" times of day.

Communicating with the Cumulus customer

Every three months the Cumulus customer receives a Cumulus account balance, Cumulus coupons worth CHF5 and a Cumulus magazine with special Cumulus offers. The points collected in these three months are paid to the customer in the form of Cumulus coupons worth CHF 5 each. A CHF5 coupon corresponds to total purchases of CHF500 – that is 50 Cumulus points. Points not divisible by 50 are automatically transferred to the next three-month period. If customers would like to know their account balance at any time during the three-month period or need further information about the Cumulus programme, they can contact the Cumulus infoline.

Cashing in the Cumulus points

The customer has two opportunities to cash in the Cumulus coupons. The coupons can be used directly to pay for purchases at any Migros business, for instance at Hotelplan for vacations, at Migrol for petrol, at Ex Libris for books and CDs or for a course at the Migros Club School. In effect, the customer is gaining a 1% discount. The other possibility is to let the value of the Cumulus coupons grow. The Cumulus magazine contains special offers from the entire range of Migros goods, for instance mountain bikes at Migros Sports & Fun, furniture at Micasa & Home, a stereo at Electronics & Future, special Secura offers, cultural events and so on. For every special offer there is a Cumulus cheque enclosed in the magazine worth between CHF10 and CHF50. The customer can claim this special discount by taking the CHF5 stickers from the Cumulus coupon and sticking them on the Cumulus cheque and fulfilling a minimum purchase requirement at the same time. Through these special offers Migros hopes to achieve increased sales in assortment areas in which it has a weak market share (cross-selling). Cumulus coupons expire two years after the issue date at the earliest. If the current Cumulus magazine does not contain any suitable offers, Cumulus coupons can be used for offers in a later Cumulus magazine.

Migros' goal is to maintain continuous contact with the customer and constantly invite him or her to a Migros point of sale. The aim is to develop the following process: the customer makes his or her purchases, receives a letter with the Cumulus coupons and the Cumulus magazine, comes back to cash in the Cumulus coupons, shops again, in three months receives a new notification and so on!

LOYALTY CARDS OFFERED BY OTHER SWISS RETAILERS

Migros was neither the first nor the only Swiss retailer to introduce a loyalty card offering benefits to its customers. Co-op, the second-largest Swiss retailer, launched its own "Cooprofit" card programme at approximately the same time. Customers using the card are eligible to benefit from special offers and rebates on selected products. In contrast to Migros' Cumulus card programme, Co-op's programme does not include the distribution of coupons and more direct mailings to customers. Instead it focuses on discounts on individual transactions. Data on consumers' shopping behaviour is not collected without their explicit consent. The Cooprofit card is accepted in various non-food outlets owned by or affiliated with Co-op, including Co-op's banking and insurance businesses, and consumer electronics and computer stores, as well as Co-op's core food retailing business.

The third major loyalty card scheme in Switzerland is a joint project called the "Shopping Bonus Card". Initiated by the department store chain Jelmoli, the card works in a way comparable to the Cumulus card, offering bonus points on purchases when displayed at the point of sale, and additionally serving as a debit card. In an innovative move, Jelmoli opened its card programme to other store chains and companies, thus enabling customers to collect "bonus points" on their purchases in any of several participating companies. In mid-

1999, 22 Swiss companies had joined this programme, among them retailers with complementary ranges of products, as well as several hotel and restaurant chains, an Internet services provider and a large insurance company. Access to a common base of cardholders encourages mutual cross-selling between the participating companies. Cardholders receive mailings about special offers on a regular basis. Beyond the benefits offered by the other cards discussed, the Shopping Bonus Card aims at offering further added value such as certain free insurance benefits valid on travel arrangements paid with the card.

THE CUMULUS CARD AND MARKET INFORMATION

What is the advantage of such cards compared with coupons?

The main advantage of the Cumulus card for Migros is the information that can be collected about customers and their shopping habits. Until recently Migros, could only generate information on the products sold – and when using their scanning system. With the Cumulus card they also know now who has purchased.

Demographic data such as name, address, household size and age is collected through the application forms. The most important data is generated when the customer uses the Cumulus card: date and time of purchase, store visited and products bought. The individual specific and purchase-specific information deliver a detailed picture of customers and their needs. Migros gains a better and more specific understanding of its customers, thereby creating a base for an individualized customer contact and service.

The information benefit which the Cumulus card is expected to generate is specified below.

Individual customer contact through customer segmentation

With the information collected, customers can be segmented and contacted according to their needs. Possible segmentation criteria are age (for instance, students, young families and senior citizens), or interests (for instance, sport, gardening and pets).

In the long term customer segment-marketing could be used to structure all marketing instruments and clearly identify customer groups. A customer segment manager, with functions similar to those of a category manager, monitors that the interests of his customers are served when arranging the assortment.

Recognizing the top customers

Through its customer loyalty card, Migros learns the names of its best customers and how much these top customers spend at Migros. It has already been ascertained that 30% of the customers make up 60% of revenues. Now it will be possible to reward these top customers for their loyalty. Migros has already organized events in stores which are open to these top customers only. Other examples of such loyalty programmes are special offers in the Cumulus magazine and top customer discussion forums concerning store policies.

At the same time it will be possible to identify those Migros customers who shop less – or not at all. These customers can then be contacted for market research reasons.

Supporting the assortment policy

Another important use of customer information is in supporting assortment policies. Special attention is given to the introduction and evaluation of new products. The following questions, for instance, can be answered:

- How are new products accepted by the consumers?
- Which customers buy the new products? (special test markets can be created by selecting customers in order to test the acceptance of new products)
- Did we acquire new customers by introducing the new product?

Supporting local subsidiary policies

In order to communicate with the customers of a local market, Migros will use its information on a local basis as well. Customers will be directly informed about changes in the assortment, renovation activities, reopenings etc.

STATUS QUO AND A VIEW OF THE FUTURE

Two and a half million Cumulus cards were in circulation within four months of the launch. Within another year, the figure exceeded three million. This was substantially more than was initially forecast. At the time of writing (in April 1999) in-house studies from the market research company, Institut für Market Analyses AG, show that 75% of Migros' customers shop with the Cumulus card, and 55% of retail revenues are generated by consumers using a Cumulus card. One in two households in Switzerland have a Cumulus card, thus providing Migros with a huge customer base. So far, their expectations for the Cumulus card have been more than fulfilled.

Nevertheless Migros still faces huge challenges: the largest of these is the efficient and intelligent exploitation of the data collected. This not only demands suitable information treatment systems, it also requires qualified personnel to analyse the data qualitatively and derive the correct marketing measures (database marketing). Customer binding will only take effect if the marketing base is correct. A customer-binding programme cannot serve to cover up basic marketing problems. Only by resolutely aiming the entire marketing effort at customer binding can the company appear credible and gain the desired success.

Questions

1. What are the critical factors for the success of the Cumulus card and of a loyalty card in general?
2. What are the benefits of the loyalty card Cumulus
   (a) for the customer?
   (b) for the company?
3. Launching loyalty cards has become very trendy in the retailing and service sector, so that one could speak about a card inflation. Because of this, a successful customer binding depends on differentiated outstanding benefits offered by the customer card. How do you judge the binding effect of the Cumulus card? What are the weak points? What measures can be taken to make the Cumulus card more integrated, attractive and understandable?

How would you design a framework for measuring and controlling the benefits resulting from the Cumulus card?
4. The main task of the Cumulus card is to get to know the customer better and to fulfil his or her needs more individually. In this context it will be a great challenge for Migros to derive the appropriate customer segments out of the flood of information. Discuss alternative customer segmentations and make concrete propositions as to how to handle them effectively.

Acknowledgements

The authors would like to thank the Migros-Genoussenschafts-Bund for the provision of documents for this case, and in particular Rolf Schutthess, Sales Manager of Migros at St Gallen, for his invaluable support, information and interest.

References and further reading

Boone, L. and Kurtz, D. (1998) *Contemporary Marketing – Wired*. Fort Worth: Dryden.
Co-op Profit Card **http://www.coop.ch/d/Card/Profitca.htm**
Evans, M. (1999) Food retailing loyalty schemes – and the Orwellian Millennium. *British Food Journal* 101(2): 132–147.
Hallier, B. (1994) Migros – Die Brücke vom Produzenten zum konsumenten. In: EHI – EuroHandelsInstitut (ed.), *Enzyklopädie des Handels*. Cologne.
Jahresbericht des Migros (1997) Genossenschafts-Bundes.
Oberst, F. (1997) *Cards & Clubs – Kunden binden, Kunden begeistern*. COP Consulting Partners Unternehmensberatung GmbH, Vortragsunterlagen.
O'Malley, L. (1998) Can loyalty schemes really build loyalty? *Marketing Intelligence and Planning* 16(1): 47–55.
Shopping Bonus Card **http://www.sbonuscard.ch**
Southworth, N. (1997) Die Tesco Clubcard. In: Haedrich, G. (ed.), *Der loyale Kunde, Ergebnisse 4*. CPC Trebd Forum, Mainz.
Tomczak, T. and Dittrich, S. (1997) *Erfolgreich Kunden binden*. Zürich.
Worthington, S. (1998) Loyalty cards and the revitalization of the town centre. *International Journal of Retail and Distribution Management*. 26(2): 68–77.

20

Customer satisfaction in emergency ambulance services: a case for empirical research

Rudolf R. Sinkovics and Barbara Stöttinger

Case	Customer satisfaction
Main focus	Health care, market liberalization
Subsidiary focus	Marketing research, non-profit-marketing
Scene	Austria, Europe-wide
Players	Health service providers, competitors, researchers
Product	Emergency services

Summary

The International Committee of the Red Cross (ICRC) is known worldwide for its international humanitarian programmes. For this it has numerous international sources of income. Donations from Austria and Germany derive from the running of emergency and ambulance services.

Competition from other organizations – both non-profit-making and private – is threatening this income source. How can the ICRC, through its agent the Austrian Red Cross, identify ways of increasing customer satisfaction and hence maintain a competitive advantage?

Introduction

This falls in the "people" area. Here we have a fascinating customer satisfaction case which one might expect to find in a book on health services or
social planning where profit maximization is not the first aim and
"consumers" are "patients". Its marketing credentials are clear, however –
a humanitarian organization known to us all is funded by the revenues of
individual national services in the health arena. These national services,
having provided effective community services at low, or zero, cost to
recipients, find they have competitors whose main aim is profit maximization. This case enables readers to look at the marketing implications of
such a scenario in more detail for emergency services in Austria. Details on
services provided and on the resources needed by the Austrian Red Cross
for this purpose are given. The decisions which have to be made by
operators in the event of an emergency are described. The costs are
spelled out and the scene set for a pilot market research project which, if
successful, will be extended to other European national members of the
International Committee of the Red Cross.

Questions for discussion cover not only the conventional areas of customer satisfaction – how would you measure it, and define and evaluate
the service and what data collection methods might you prefer? Readers
are also invited to think through strategies for dealing with a situation
where any successful strategy will almost inevitably lead to increased
competition from profit-maximizing rivals.

KEYWORDS

Health care, emergency services, liberalization of markets, non-
profit-marketing, ethics, marketing research.

Case

INTRODUCTION

Whenever news flashes report on disastrous events such as military
conflicts or natural and environmental catastrophes (such as floods or
droughts), we can rely on the immediate reaction of the International
Committee of the Red Cross (ICRC) to alleviate the big problems.
This extraordinary humanitarian commitment and the capability for
instantaneous help is facilitated through the ICRC's network of

affiliate member organizations throughout the world and its well-established organizational and financial infrastructure. (For further detail see Appendix.)

The ICRC is funded through its national member organizations which themselves generate revenue through the delivery of various social and health care services to their local and national communities. Some of these services, such as rescue efforts after avalanche accidents, reunifying families, assistance in natural catastrophes or wars, are highly unprofitable on the international as well as on the national level due to their enormous set-up and maintenance costs. If it were not for the organization's humanitarian mission, many of these demanding services would not be offered. However, this implies that highly profitable services have to subsidize others. As a result, the ICRC is constantly concerned with the national and the overall profitability of the services portfolio.

For this reason, the ICRC has launched several tracking studies to improve profitability in its different strategic business units such as ambulance and rescue services, general health care services, administration of blood donations and first aid classes. "Ambulance and Rescue Services" are particularly well established and financially successful in Germany and Austria, where they account for more than 50% of total revenue. The Austrian Red Cross management attributes this success to widespread service availability and closeness to the customers' needs.

In order to remain profitable in this promising service area, the Austrian Red Cross was asked to conduct a pilot study which would identify ways of increasing customer satisfaction and retention. If research results are promising, the design of the study will be transferred to other European countries.

THE DEVELOPMENT OF THE MARKET FOR SOCIAL AND HEALTH CARE SERVICES

Social and health care services are "products" of increasing potential. One major reason lies in the significant demographic and social changes which Austria like many other European countries has been facing over the last decades (Österreichisches Statistisches Zentralamt 1998).

- The traditional form of family relations has been changing into its smallest form – the nuclear family (parents and children, single parents with children). While in the past the extended family provided personal care for elderly family members, this need for personal assistance has increasingly to be sourced out to professional organizations.

- Additional support for this trend towards professional assistance in social and health care comes from the increasing participation of women in the active workforce. Time constraints now prevent them from offering these unpaid services. Due to the lack of family care, elderly or physically impaired people are now having to live either on their own or in nursing homes.

- This situation is aggravated even more by increasing life expectancy throughout Austria and other highly industrialized countries in Europe. Demographic forecasts for the year 2030 project the share of over-60-year-olds at around 35% and more of the total population, compared with around 20% today.

At the same time, governmental agencies are trying to relieve the already strained social services and health care budgets which are already stretched by redirecting funds from inpatient to outpatient care. For the Austrian Red Cross, this means that the demand for ambulance and emergency services will increase even further.

Despite its outstanding market position and consequent sound financial background, the Austrian Red Cross is under continual pressure from new entrants, who have been lured into offering similar transportation services because of perceived promising market potential. Whilst not forsaking its humanitarian mission, it nevertheless is imperative for the Austrian Red Cross to run its core business as financially successfully as possible and stay ahead of competition.

EMERGENCY AND AMBULANCE SERVICES – AN INTERESTING "PRODUCT"

Emergency and ambulance services are more complex than they might appear. The services spectrum ranges from simple prescheduled transportation services (transportation to home after outpatient hospital treatment, transportation to and from doctors' offices, etc.) to emergency operations after severe accidents, which require extensive medical equipment and sophisticated know-how. To serve these different service demands, the Austrian Red Cross uses different types of ambulance vehicles. Depending on the specific nature of the services task (serious accident, prescheduled transportation service, etc.), they differ in technical and medical equipment as well as in personnel resources supplied. Table 20.1 gives an overview of the fleet.

Initial contact with customers is usually established via telephone, either by the patient or her/his relatives themselves or medical institutions (hospitals, doctors). In the case of a serious accident on the street, either passers-by, the police or fire brigades order emergency transport. Telephone calls are answered by a highly trained operator. This job has a high stress level and carries significant responsibility. The operator has to evaluate, categorize and rank different transportation requests according to their urgency. Based on these categorizations, the appropriate emergency vehicle is directed to the patient and the actual service is carried out.

FINANCIAL ASPECTS OF EMERGENCY AND AMBULANCE SERVICES

The operator's decision as to which vehicle to send out for transportation services depends on a precise assessment of customer demand. As different types of vehicles imply different costs, this choice significantly influences the financial revenue situation of the Austrian Red Cross.

This effect is due to the particular framework for reimbursement of transportation services by governmental health care organizations. For example, for emergency transport after a severe accident, the Austrian Red Cross receives a lump sum, which hardly ever covers the cost incurred. In most cases, the actual costs for this sophisticated service are at least four or five times higher than the amount reimbursed. In addition, consumers of ambulance transportation services are not liable to pay compensation under the current legal situation.

Less sophisticated transportation services which do not require extensive medical care or a doctor accompanying the ambulance are

TABLE 20.1   Equipment of transportation vehicles, Austria 1999

Vehicles	Personnel resources	Technical equipment	Approximate initial costs
Emergency doctor's car (NAW)	one doctor, two ambulance men	Electrocardiogram monitor, oxygen mask, respirator, infusion apparatus, container for severed body parts	ATS 1 800 000
Ambulance (RTW)	two ambulance men	In many cases the equipment is equivalent to the equipment of a NAW	ATS 1 000 000
Ambulance service (KTW)	two ambulance men	Vacuum mattress, medicaments, oxygen, patient seat, patient carrier	ATS 600 000
Ambulance service support vehicle (BKTW)	one ambulance man	Portable first-aid equipment	ATS 350 000

ATS, Austrian schillings.

Source: in-house. Reproduced with permission.

financed through a variable amount of money depending on the length of the transport (rate per kilometre) and the type of vehicle used. Due to the better cost/reward situation, these services produce the substantial, financial surplus necessary to compensate for emergency services' deficit.

With regard to the new competitors, which are mostly privately owned companies, the following has to be noted: their profit maximizing strategy leads to a limited service range covering the most lucrative transportation services, such as less sophisticated ambulance services particularly in urban areas, while expensive ones like emergency services and services in rural areas remain with the Austrian Red Cross service portfolio.

In order to achieve a more demand- and customer-oriented marketing approach, the Austrian Red Cross is collaborating on this pilot project with a group of researchers at Vienna University. The following questions arise during the planning meeting.

Questions

1. How would you measure customer satisfaction with the Austrian Red Cross ambulance and emergency services?
2. Who would you define as customers of the emergency and ambulance services?
3. Which method of data collection would you propose?
4. Which difficulties might occur in the data collection process?
5. Based on the humanitarian mission of the Austrian Red Cross, which strategies would you suggest to cope with private competitors specializing only in the most lucrative niches (such as transportation services)?
6. You want to replicate the study in a different country setting (your home country or any other country of your choice). Your research goal is to compare research findings across the countries involved. Which adaptations to the research design are required to replicate the study?

References

Badelt, C. (ed.) (1997) *Handbuch der Nonprofit Organization, Strukturen und Management*. Vienna: Schäffer Poeschel.

Becker, J. (1998) *Marketing-Konzeption: Grundlagen strategischen Marketing-Managements*, 6. A. Munich: Vahlen.

Churchill, G.J. (1995) *Marketing Research. Methodological Foundations*, 6th edn. London: Dryden.

Hannagan, T. (1992) *Marketing for the Non-profit Sector*. Baskingstoke: Macmillan.

Haug, H. (1994) *Menschlichkeit für alle: die Weltbewegung des Roten Kreuzes und des Roten Halbmondes*. Bern: Institut Henry Dunant.

Hunt, S.D., Chonko, L.B. and Wilcox, J.B. (1984) Ethical problems of marketing researchers. *Journal of Marketing* 21 (August): 309–324.

Kotler, P. and Eduardo, R.L. (1989) *Social Marketing: Strategies for Changing Public Behavior*. New York: Free Press.

Marte, C. (1995) *Österreichisches Rotes Kreuz, Broschüre mit Grundsätzen, Leitbild und Schwerpunkten der Rotkreuz-Arbeit*. Vienna: Pressel-Druck.

Österreichisches Statistisches Zentralamt (1998) *Statistische Nachrichten*, 53. No. 9, September.

Rados, D.L. (1981) *Marketing for Non-profit Organizations*. Boston: Auburn House.

Tschan, E. (1990) Die strategische Ausrichtung einer Non-Profit-Organization am Beispiel des Schweizer Roten Kreuzes. Dissertation der Hochschule St Gallen.

Appendix: The International Committee of the Red Cross (ICRC)

HISTORY

It all started in 1859 on the battlefield of the Italian town of Solferino, when the Swiss businessman Henry Dunant was profoundly touched by the agony of thousands of wounded soldiers left to die without medical services. He immediately organized locals for assistance, insisting that soldiers on both sides should be cared for. His initiative soon led to the foundation of a formal organization – the International Committee of the Red Cross. Today, the ICRC has concluded agreements with more than 50 states worldwide. These national societies embody the work and the principles within the Global Network of the International Federation of Red Cross and Red Crescent Societies.

MISSION

The International Committee of the Red Cross (ICRC) is an impartial, neutral and independent organization whose exclusively humanitarian mission is to protect the lives and dignity of victims of war and internal violence and to provide them with assistance. It directs and coordinates the international relief activities conducted by the Movement in situations of conflict. It also endeavours to prevent suffering by promoting and strengthening humanitarian law and universal humanitarian principles.

ACTIVITIES

The ICRC operates in several distinct areas:

- *Visits to detainees*: ICRC delegates visited more than 200 000 detainees in over 1500 places of detention in more than 50 countries
- *Restoration of family ties*: another main area of concern is to reunite family members who were split up by conflict, disturbances or tensions. In 1998, the ICRC collected almost 307 000 messages and distributed more than 295 000
- *Assistance*: in 1998, relief supplies such as food, clothing, blankets or tents with a value of $80 million and medical assistance worth $22 million were distributed in 52 countries worldwide
- *Surgery/care for the disabled*: the ICRC runs and supplies several hospitals in Africa and Asia and assists medical facilities in countries with need worldwide

Figure A20.1 shows how ICRC funds are distributed.

FUNDING

The ICRC relies mainly on four different sources of voluntary contributions: governments, supranational organizations such as the European Union, public sources and the National Red Cross and Red Crescent Societies (Figure A20.2).

THE ICRC AND NATIONAL SOCIETIES

In order to accomplish its activities, the ICRC maintains close contact with its National Red Cross and Red Crescent Societies. This close relationship allows for an efficient and quick reaction by the ICRC and its national societies when international interventions become necessary. In addition, the ICRC provides technical assistance by supporting the National Societies' dissemination programmes and by contributing to the training of their staff.

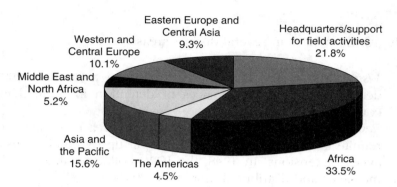

FIGURE A20.1   ICRC expenditure by region 1997 (total 702.5 million Swiss francs) (including contributions in kind and services). Source: "ICRC: Answers to your questions". Reproduced with permission of ICRC.

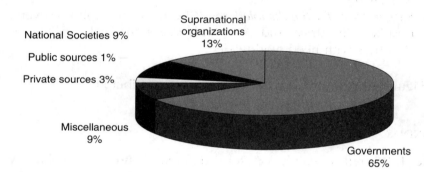

FIGURE A20.2   ICRC budget, by source, 1997. (Total budget for 1997: 698.1 million francs.) Source: "The ICRC worldwide in 1998", March 1999. Reproduced with permission of ICRC.

THE NATIONAL SOCIETIES

In its home country, each National Society supports government authorities in humanitarian matters – primarily by backing up the military medical services in time of conflict. In addition, each National Society may carry out specific activities in accordance with the Fundamental Principles such as collection of blood, training of first-aid workers and nurses, running of dispensaries or hospitals, and providing aid to the disabled, young people, and the elderly.

THE AUSTRIAN RED CROSS

The Austrian Red Cross (ÖRK) is one of the ICRC's National Societies. According to its Fundamental Principles, the ÖRK is carrying out its social services in the Austrian community. During the past 50 years of peace, its activities have been mainly concentrated on emergency and ambulance services, health care and social services such as first-aid courses, meals on wheels, day and home care for the elderly or the Austrian blood donation system.

In 1996, the ÖRK provided 17 745 000 hours of service to the community with its 5166 employees and 33 550 volunteers. Translated into financial terms, this equals ATS2.7 bn (almost £200 million; based on a minimum hourly wage of ATS260).

THE AUSTRIAN HEALTH CARE SYSTEM

The Austrian health care system provides universal coverage to its citizens through the government-sponsored social insurance carrier. This socialized, "cradle-to-grave health care system" is financed through contributions by employers, employees and taxes. In Austria, the average employee salary contribution is about 13%. Unemployed people, retired people and citizens on welfare get government-paid coverage. Payments to doctors, the hospital or other health care providers (such as the Austrian Red Cross) go directly to the health care provider.

Source: **http://www.icrc.org/** (27 July 1999); **http://www.red-cross.or.at/** (27 July 1999); **http://www.ifrc.org/** (28 July 1999); Floh, A. and Kopietz P. (1998) Die Messung der Qualität unfreiwilliger Dienstleistungen, Diplomarbeit, Wirtschaftsuniversität, Vienna.

Index of keywords by case number